Play It By Trust

A guide to ethical digital marketing

By Thom Poole
© 2005-08

Written by Thomas F Poole © 2005-08 Thom Poole

First edition published by Lulu in 2007
Second edition & paperback published by Lulu in 2008

ISBN 978-1-4092-0392-6

To my wife Emma
for your support throughout this project

Contents

Introduction

The ethics debate is raging in the marketing industry, with over exaggeration 'spinning' out of control, and the over abundance of spam hitting our inboxes.

The ethics depend on the culture in which we live, and are moving targets, changing with experiences and fashions.

This book is split in to the strategic and tactical considerations around the ethical framework of your marketplace, and aspirations and values of your customers. Your customers should be at the forefront of strategic development, and their ethics and moral codes should be guiding factors in your tactical planning and methods of conducting an ethical digital marketing campaign.

It is, however, important to understand what ethics and the electronic media mean. With the incestuous rise in spam it is difficult to see that this media can ever be an ethical medium, and that any activity in the media could be ethical.

This book was originally born after publication of a dissertation on "Data privacy and the marketing art of the opt-in." The title of the book came from a visit to the contemporary art museum in Budapest one wet and cold January, where a sculpture is on display by Yoko Ono. It comprises of a white table, two white chairs and a white chess board and two sets of white chess pieces – it is entitled "Play It By Trust."

A – Strategic ethics

1. Background

1.1　What is ethical marketing?

Modern business thinks that ethical activity involves developing a Corporate Social Responsibility (CSR) programme and policy, how wrong they can be. Some years ago there was a move towards an enhanced CSR called Corporate Citizenship. Corporate Citizenship was a theory that the company would be a key player in their local communities (the extent of the locality was dependent on the company's definition).

The Corporate Citizenship Company has identified three key levels at which CSR issues arise. In descending order of importance they are:

- The basic values, policy and practices of a company's owned and operated businesses
- The management of social issues within the value chain by business partners, from raw material acquisition to product disposal
- The wider contributions made by a company, and increasingly its stakeholders, to community development and resolving social and environmental problems around the world

These levels are illustrated in the diagram below.

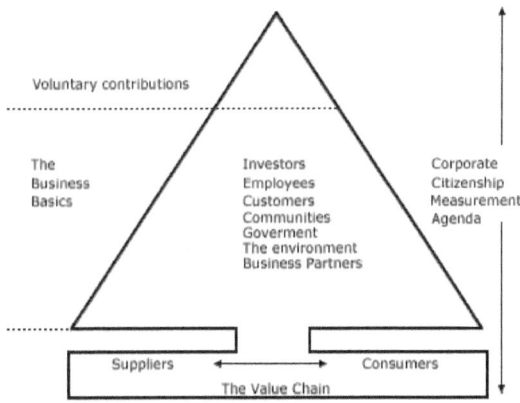

Figure 1. The three components of corporate citizenship[i]

Corporate Citizenship or CSR are only one aspect of ethics. Ethics are a system of moral principles, rules or standards that govern the conduct of members of a group. Ethical codes of conduct approach human behaviour from a philosophical standpoint by stressing objectively defined, but essentially idealistic, standards (or laws) of right and wrong, good and evil; and virtue and vice such as those applicable to the practices of lawyers and doctors[ii].

Personal or societal ethics are the moral code by which we live – they rule everyone, some more strictly than others. To understand the personal and corporate ethical issues in marketing, we must first understand the drivers for the ethics themselves; how are they formed, communicated and maintained. Corporate ethics are, however, not just limited to marketing, as finance, sales and other activities are all guided by ethical codes. Ethics are a major element in the formation and maintenance of trust.

Ethics can be formed both positively and negatively, even from the same source, the examples being used to guide people in their use, or abuse. Most of our personal ethics have been formed by religion, our environment, education and people around us. Over the years each society has been shaped by religious teachings – in the Judaeo-Christian world this has the Ten Commandments as its religious basis.

The business ethics community has some soul searching ahead of it, argued awarding winning producer and author, Jon Entine. Is it about outward-focused social vision, as represented by many vocal leaders? Or is it about ethics? Putting out a quality product at reasonable prices; treating employees, vendors, franchisees, and investors fairly; acting responsibly toward the local environment and community; and, most of all, embracing transparency in operations and accountability to critics, internal and external? This can be seen in the simplified structure shown in Figure 2.

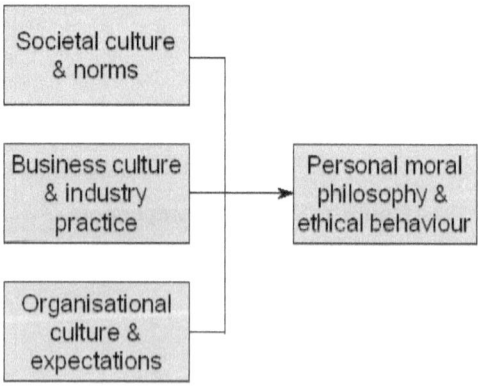

Figure 2. The framework for understanding ethical behaviour[iii]

Ethics, like democracy, are a lot easier in theory than in practice. As an example, let's look at the proliferation of codes of conduct and mission statements that have been drafted in the wake of the American 'Kathie Lee Gifford' fiasco over foreign sweatshops. The Gifford 'scandalette', as helpful as it has been in shining needed light on the complicated issue of foreign sourcing, may also leave us with a not-very-progressive legacy if we're not careful. Entine concludes by identifying that character is demonstrated by actions, not by intentions, is the only reliable measure of corporate ethics[iv].

John McClenahen, senior editor at IndustryWeek, poses the 'ethical' question of a company operating in France, downloading Oracle software from a server in California and paying for the package through its British office to take advantage of a lower tax rate. He asks if this is ethical, despite it being legal? He also poses the question whether a company that links its website with other retail sites has an ethical obligation to disclose any business relationships it has with the firms[v]? I don't think there is an answer here – it really comes back to the question of customer perceptions, and what would they think about the disclosure of the information should it become public knowledge.

A negative influence on ethics can also shape a community, and therefore marketplace. An example of this is prejudice, whereby a part of the community or environment is deemed unclean, problematic or criminal. This can lead communities to develop in certain directions where abuse of the unwanted elements is excluded from ethical behaviour. The persecution of the Jews in Nazi Germany, or the persecution of Gypsy's in Eastern Europe, are both recent examples of this. Unfortunately, there are all too many more examples.

In marketing terms we must understand the drivers for ethical behaviour amongst our target audience in terms of their buying and repeat purchase behaviours, so as to exploit possible advantages over our competitors. Marketers have a role to play in reinforcing, and to some extent, policing the ethical perceptions of the market where it can be used as a competitive advantage. The religious, educational and legal systems are the key drivers of personal ethical behaviour, and therefore, to some extent, of corporate ethics, so these systems must be appeased – just look at the way the fast-food industry is trying to get in line with current government thinking about healthy eating. They are being proactive on the whole so as to reduce the effects on their industry.

Ethical marketing is the current goal of all companies in a desperate attempt to access their markets. The increase in theft and unsavoury advertising now leads many customers to be wary of the activities of companies, especially multinationals. Naomi Klein's book – No Logo[vi] - has increased the pressure on the multinationals by highlighting unsavoury activities, especially around use of third world manufacturing, including the use of child labour.

1.2   What is digital marketing?

Digital marketing is the regarded as the electronic version of the marketing profession. In real terms, very little changes when marketing online, the channel is just more direct and interactive. In pre-Internet markets, companies paid handsomely for professional salesmanship, but nowadays, much of the interaction can be automated, and customer's demands have increased accordingly.

Having been trained as a full-mix marketer, I would disagree with the thinking that digital marketing is a separate discipline, but I would also say the same of public relations (PR) and direct marketing, etc. There are of course differences between on- and offline marketing, but a thorough offline marketer would make few mistakes in the online environment.

We understand digital or e-media as encompassing all 'electronic' communications channels to the customer. Electronic or e-media integrates functions, and provides seamless usability for authors and users, as well as adapting to systems and time, and includes the Internet, e-mail, Instant Messaging and Chat, mobile phones (using messaging services such as Short Messaging Service - SMS) and, increasingly interactive digital television (iDTV).

The World Wide Web (www), the main driver for most e-media, was established when the first computers were connected, or networked, and files shared. During the late 1940's, computing grew and the US Military and academia in general saw the potential of sharing information. At the time, this involved huge computers that took up a whole room for each computer and file with very little power and very limited information sharing!

Sir Tim Berners-Lee is accredited with developing the 'modern' Internet, stating his vision that it would become a global information space where information would be stored on computers everywhere was linked and available to anyone anywhere[vii]. It grew in prominence in the early 1990's throughout academic institutions, predominantly in the USA. One of the main drivers for the growth of the Internet was the launch of the personal computer, initially by Apple, and then the IBM Personal Computer or PC.

The spread of user-friendly computer interfaces took place concurrently with an amalgamation of modern media into a converging digital source. Professor Nicholas Negroponte, of the MIT Media Lab, is best known for his efforts to publicise and hasten this convergence:

"All communication technologies are suffering a joint metamorphosis, which can only be understood properly if treated as a single subject, and only advanced properly if treated as a single craft"[viii].

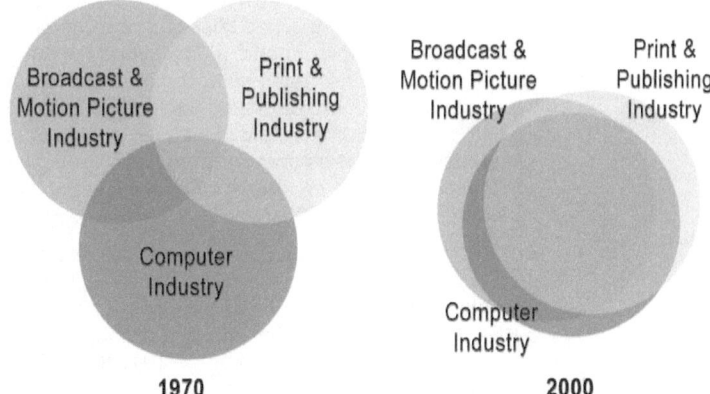

Figure 3. Negroponte's case for the Media Laboratory at MIT[ix]

Used in isolation, digital marketing is a proven advertising and interaction channels, but as has been shown in recent campaigns; a consistent, integrated approach, combining a number of these channels provides a very effective and longer lasting impression.

Websites, call centres and iDTV are all inbound marketing channels whereby customers initiate the interaction. These are channels that are difficult to regulate, unless the barriers are there to ring-fence a particular type of personal or unsavoury content and the barrier is proactive. Most modern web browsers now incorporate barriers to this.

E-mail, messaging and offline direct and mass marketing are all examples of outbound marketing that can to a certain extent, be targeted to more receptive audiences.

Digital marketing therefore encompasses the Internet, direct outbound marketing, and interactive advertising. The Internet is used for the following:

- Brochureware
- Sales
- Support
- Administration
- Procurement
- Education
- Training
- Tracking
- Entertainment
- Information/News

The Internet is a shop window for a company's products and services, providing the catalogue, shop checkout and customer support to customers – twenty-four hours a day. When the Internet first started attracting companies, it was quite common to see scanned images of the corporate brochure displayed behind hyperlinks. Whilst this view is horrific given the current state of web development, it must be remembered that web pages in those days were generally plain text, with no graphics, so the idea of using typeset pictures was not badly intended.

As security improved, and the access to the Internet increased, companies started to experiment with the media and explore new ways to exploit this channel to the marketplace, be it to educate the customers, provide formal or informal training, tracking of products or processes (an example would be the parcel tracking that delivery companies offer), or the growth of online newspapers – either the formal newspapers (covering mainstream stories) to the informal blogging (web logs or online diaries).

When I first started working in the late 1980's, we had a typing pool, ledgers were compiled by hand and print layouts were developed by cutting and pasting (in a physical way). When I tell younger colleagues this, they look as though I come from another planet – since then, of course, typing pools and secretaries have become extinct and every executive now needs to be a typist and typesetter on top of their day-to-day roles.

Desk research can now be carried out immediately and actions transmitted as quickly. This does not mean that research specialists have ceased to exist, as they now also use the Internet to conduct their research projects.

The Internet has now also spread to mobile devices, such as mobile phones and personal digital assistant devices (PDA's). Internet kiosks and cafes have enabled people to access the Internet on the move, without their own devices – increasing the reach of digital marketing, both on the mass marketing level in websites, etc, and to individuals via their personal e-mail accounts.

Segmentation

Segmentation is as important online as it is offline, although as mentioned, it is potentially more difficult to prevent untargeted audiences visiting your website. One way that websites tailor their offering to the visiting customer is via the use of customer relationship management (CRM) systems that operate in 'real-time', or as a reaction to the last action of the customer.

e-CRM systems are complex platforms that assess the customer's click profile (the pages viewed, and the order that they were viewed), the static profile (any information the customer has given you, for example during registration), and any transactional profiles.

The most quoted example of this is the Amazon website (**www.amazon.com**), in which a product (or indeed a product group) viewed will start an analysis to see what others who viewed that page or product group then viewed and/or bought. In this way a comprehensive cross- and up-sell process can be started, making the most of the interaction. If you do not yet have an Amazon account, do not let this stop you. Try it out by browsing some pages, and then find the option for the personalised pages.

The downside of this type of system is that every page you view (or your account views, if someone logs on using your details) will build a picture of your buying (reading, listening, etc) profile. For example, I bought my niece a children's book and Amazon now thinks that I am a regular children's book buyer, which could be a good reminder when it gets close to her birthday, but otherwise it overwrites potential products that I would be interested in.

To overcome this, many systems also employ a 'persona' profile. Personas are customer profiles as they change in the course of the day, week, month and year. The example I use is for the mobile phone data market where a business person wants stock prices during the week, but come 3pm on a Saturday, their persona changes to 'Football Nut', and by timing the relevant products to the more receptive times may help in selling football related products to that individual.

Friendship

CRM has 'relationships' at its heart, but many of the automated systems fail to address the relationship thanks to an inability to have any empathy with the customers. When I worked as a salesman, my manager used to quote 'people buy from their friends'. This is a useful analogy as in face-to-face selling; personality and rapport have a major factor in success or failure. The supermarket, whilst still officially a 'people' environment, has a different interactive requirement in that products must be packaged and displayed in such a way to make them attractive to the customer, and encourage the self-service and selection of the products.

In an electronic environment, the customer's power grows to new levels. The customer is in control of which shop, almost anywhere in the world, that they wish to shop in, and what information they are prepared to provide during the transaction. There is not even a shelf-stacker available to point them in the right direction to find a product, service or information – everything must be done within the design of the website.

Systems such as e-CRM platforms overlie this and try to provide the personal service back to the transaction. Most systems learn from their interaction, but they all obviously start with very little information. A major limitation in e-CRM systems has been the lack of investment in the setting up of the software, and its ongoing maintenance. If the system is trying to learn the wrong traits, or reacting to the wrong triggers, the relationship may be so damaged that the sale does not even take place.

This is where trust fails. In the course of researching this book, the focus changed from an ethical debate to a debate about trust, hence the title of this book. Trust underlies everything a company does. The quote about friendship selling products works because it involves trust – though when confronted by a salesperson, I cannot say that I have any trust in them, but if I had no confidence or empathy with them, it is unlikely that I would buy from them.

Brands also have a character, as built up by the branding experts within a company (another artificial segmentation of the marketing profession), and this becomes the driver/s that customers relate to when dealing with the company, even via a third party. This branding is even more important online as it is on a medium that during its short existence, has gained notoriety as being an insecure and fraudulent channel. The trust customers have in the brand will overcome much of the bad publicity the medium on which the brand operates.

Trust is explored in more detail in a later chapter.

Electronic marketing communications

The various marketing communications (or Marcoms) channels have been mentioned, and in the online environment, they have benefited from the speed and interactivity offered. There is, however, a problem in that so many more messages are being presented to customers, many of which are unsolicited, or spam messages. Spam destroys trust, and is discussed in more detail in chapter 2.

But as the electronic media is inundated with unwanted messages, so it develops new ways to address customers directly. In the 2002 Steven Spielberg film, Minority Report, the main character, played by Tom Cruise, walks along a subway hallway. The systems used to identify people in this film uses retinal recognition, and using this advertisers display personalised, holographic advertisements as the customer passes by. These adverts are both audio and video transmissions, which in the short time they are used in the film can already irritate some viewers.

When I present trust marketing issues, I show a clip from the film Minority Report and I ask the audience if this is a scary image of the future, or marketing 'nirvana'? Many responses show that it is a bit of both. The extreme personalisation is the goal of every direct marketer, especially online where the interaction is so valuable. On the negative side, however, they all feel that such personalisation could and probably would erode trust in their brand if wrongly implemented.

This is also an issue today; we could get too personal and scare the customers away from the brand. In the mobile phone market, it is possible to triangulate the position of a customer's mobile phone. If you phone a location based service (LBS), such as a traffic reporting service, it will start by saying, "you are near Manchester…" for example. If the mobile phone advertisers were to say "We know that you are near the cinema – why not go and see the latest Spielberg?", would you think that this is clever marketing, or would you look around to find out who is spying on you?

Seth Godin, in his book[x] talks about interruption marketing. This is the term he gives to mass marketing, although any badly targeted direct marketing is probably a greater interruption thanks to the delivery mechanisms of e-mail, post, text messaging, etc. He advocates a permission-only marketing practice in which customers invite companies to interact with them.

In the face of the increasing tide of spam, ISP's and manufacturers are examining ways to limit, if not eliminate, spam! Microsoft have suggested a postage fee system, which has not been well received by the market, especially as Trojan viruses have infected home computers and are triggered to send spam, which would use and spend the owner's "postage."

Godin quotes the American Management Association who says that more than half of all business executives rely on e-mail, though I would question how successful the other half are. He also quoted a Catholic bishop from New York who said, 'If Jesus were walking the earth today, I'm convinced He would have an e-mail address.'

Another potential solution is very much aligned to Godin's ideas, namely the use of white lists. This is where a customer will load the e-mail addresses, in this case, of their friends, acquaintances and trusted suppliers. This list would be held on the server, and any unsolicited messages would be rejected. From a consumer's perspective, this is a great solution, but marketers would then be prevented from legitimately cold calling customers. But coming back to the element of trust – a marketer should build trust in the brand so that customers want to set up the domain in their personal white list, and keep it active in the list.

Summary

Digital marketing covers the electronic communications mix, mainly associated with the World Wide Web and is now an established component of the overall marketing mix of a company or brand, in terms of communications, sales and delivery.

It is clear that companies that use the medium effectively benefit from better customer information and increased interactivity, but the mistrust that currently exists on the Internet, means that many trailblazing marketers are actually building trust in the medium as well as the brand.

The speed of the medium can also destroy a distrusted brand as speed of mouse, as opposed speed of mouth can travel further and faster making or, normally, breaking a brand in chat rooms or on bulletin boards.

An integrated approach is the best use of a marketing budget, and well-targeted e-communications can build not only a brand reputation and trustworthiness, but also profit, as it also benefits from a cheaper communications medium.

1.3　Can digital marketing be ethical?

In the past five years or so, spam has become an increasing problem to web users, and to online marketers. The rise of this spam increases the noise over which marketers must reach to communicate with their customers.

The spam is unsolicited and therefore is seen as unethical, but we should first take a long at look at what spam is. Whilst this will be explored in detail in the next chapter, it is worth noting that spam is an unsolicited communication, normally fro something that a customer does not want, has never had any interest in, or is utterly inappropriate.

Junk mail used to be the evil of marketing practice, with tonnes of unwanted paper falling through letterboxes each day. The costs of this were thought to be prohibitive, despite the annual increases in this type of marketing. Digital marketing has offered companies a cheaper, direct means of communicating with their customers, or potential customers. The issues, however, remain the same – the message and offer should be relevant to the customer, and if it is not, the message is classified as spam.

Spam is therefore deemed unethical. The ethical message is one the customer expects, is relevant to their requirements or desires, and is delivered at an appropriate time. Therefore, a company that has previously delivered 'ethical' messages may be seen as sending spam when they send a message about an unwanted product or service, or at an inappropriate time.

That is the negative view of marketing ethics. It does, however, mean that companies can be ethical with their digital marketing practices. The technology does exist to allow a company to build accurate profiles of their customers, and therefore to deliver a relevant, timely message. This book provides a guide to building a trusted brand and conduct ethical digital marketing campaigns, so if it were not possible for digital marketing to be ethical, this would be a very short book!

2.   Ethical framework

2.1 Ethical framework

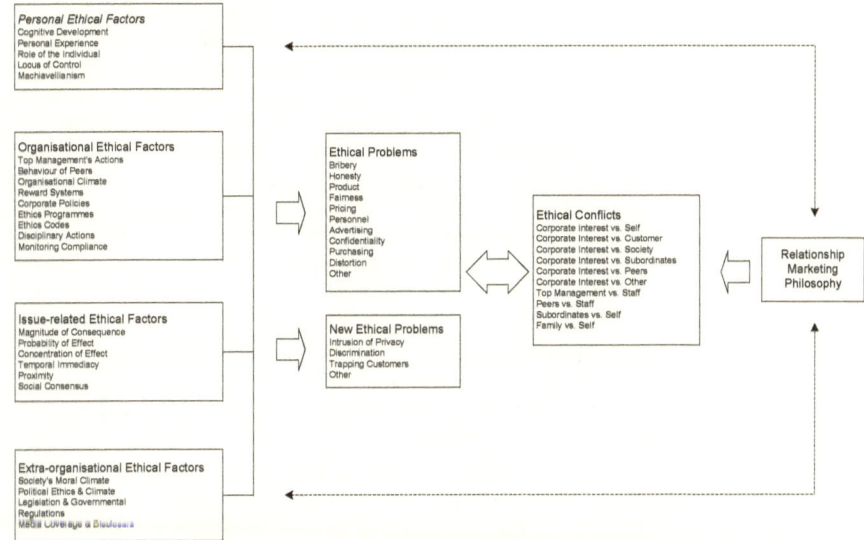

Figure 4. Ethics & relationship marketing[xi]

Figure 4 demonstrates the multi-faceted world of ethics, covering personal, organisational, community and event-triggered ethical viewpoints, and how they all relate to relationship marketing. The lists cannot be seen to conclusive, but they do form a good foundation to understanding ethics.

Personal ethical factors – according to Kavell's model (Figure 4), personal factors include cognitive development, personal experiences, the role of the individual, locus of control and Machiavellianism.

Stages of cognitive development. Jean Piaget (1896-1980) identified four stages in cognitive development[xii]:

1. **Sensorimotor stage** (Infancy). In this period (which has 6 stages), intelligence is demonstrated through motor activity without the use of symbols. Knowledge of the world is limited (but developing) because it is based on physical interactions/experiences. Children acquire object permanence at about 7 months of age (memory). Physical development (mobility) allows the child to begin developing new intellectual abilities. Some symbolic (language) abilities are developed at the end of this stage

2. **Pre-operational stage** (Toddler and early childhood). In this period, intelligence is demonstrated using symbols, language use matures, and memory and imagination are developed, but thinking is done in an illogical, irreversible manner. Egocentric thinking predominates

3. **Concrete operational stage** (Elementary and early adolescence). In this stage (characterised by 7 types of conservation: number, length, liquid, mass, weight, area, volume), intelligence is demonstrated through logical and systematic manipulation of symbols related to concrete objects. Operational thinking develops (mental actions that are reversible). Egocentric thought diminishes

4. **Formal operational** stage (Adolescence and adulthood). In this stage, intelligence is demonstrated through the logical use of symbols related to abstract concepts. Early in the period there is a return to egocentric thought. Only 35% of US high school graduates in industrialised countries obtain formal operations; many people do not think formally during adulthood

Personal experiences – These are all the experiences a marketer and company executives gather whilst conducting business, and the experiences that the customers gain from transacting with the company and its competitors.

Role of the individual – This has different implications for different scenarios and depends on the role of society and how the individuals interact within it.

Locus of control - Rotter (1966) devised a locus of control personality test to assess the extent to which an individual possesses internal or external reinforcement beliefs[xiii].

Machiavellianism - Business ethics research, while focusing on a number of individual character variables, has typically investigated these factors in isolation. What has been absent is an emphasis on a fixed constellation of characteristics that form a personality type. The field of clinical psychology provides a contribution with regard to the issue of ethical behaviour. One aspect of research that has received increasing attention is the study of psychopathy. The psychopathic personality is often associated with behaviours that, to most, are questionable from an ethical and moral perspective[xiv].

Organisational ethical factors – include top management actions, the behaviour of peers and the organisational climate and rewards and disciplinary system. Corporate policies and the ethical codes and programmes and how they are monitored.

Board actions – The actions of the board can directly influence the direction the ethics of a company can take, and as such, are a vital factor in the ethical actions within a marketplace.

Organisational climate – As a by-product of the board actions, the organisational climate will affect the ethical view of a company and its employees.

Behaviour of peers – The actions and perceptions of the employees obviously determine the organisational climate and the actions and perceptions of their peers. Ethical companies can be guided, but are only as ethical as the sum of their parts.

Rewards & disciplinary systems – It is a perennial issue whether it is easier to manage by the carrot or the stick – namely by means of rewards or threats. In terms of ethics, a healthy mix of both should be explored.

Corporate policies, codes and programmes – Companies that communicate their policies clearly and succinctly are more likely to encourage the correct behaviour amongst their employees. A popular policy amongst many companies is the development of Corporate Social Responsibility programmes, which was discussed earlier in this chapter.

Monitoring – Policies are only as good as the controls in place to ensure that they are upheld, so monitoring is a vital aspect of an organisations ethical policy.

Issue-related ethical factors – Issues facing organisations and marketers within those organisations include the magnitude of the consequences, probability and concentration of the effect, immediacy, proximity and social consensus of the actions (or inactions).

Magnitude of consequences – The magnitude of Enron's failure, and the knock-on effects show the dramatic aspects of getting it all wrong. It could be argued that a 'white lie' would not hurt, and therefore is permissible – i.e. a matter of the magnitude.

Probability and concentration of effect – If something bad is more likely to happen, a company and its employees may be less likely to want to take the risk. If the risk is acceptable and manageable, it may be that the organisation is happy to bend the ethical rules.

Immediacy & proximity – If a risk is imminent and close to home, either geographically or within an important market, it is likely that the organisation will defer unethical activities for fear of alienating their customers.

Social consensus – Ethics are determined by the society in which we live and trade, so if an ethical policy contradicts local standards and expectations, social consensus will lead an organisation and its employees to adopt a stricter or alternative policy.

Extra-organisational ethical factors – The factors outside the organisation that affect the ethical framework include society's moral climate, the political ethics and regulations. The media coverage and disclosure policies also play a part.

Society's moral climate – Morals and ethics are developed by society and so the moral climate is an important gauge for companies to ensure that they keep the public on their side.

Political ethics and climate – In the UK we have been plagued with political sleaze since the 1980's, developing a climate of distrust towards politicians. Some countries allow activities that others would think are unethical, for example, Switzerland removed the tax exemption for bribes only in the late 1990's.

Legislation & governmental regulations – Governments can influence the ethical framework of a market, and can pass laws to force compliance, although these may be contrary to public opinion.

Media coverage and disclosure – You can probably identify the politics of the newspapers you buy, and of the other media you are exposed to. Some will disclose their preferences, whilst others demonstrate their politics and ethical/moral standpoint with their editorials.

Ethical problems – These factors exist within the society in which the organisation operates. They include bribery, fairness confidentiality, distortion and honesty.

Bribery – To bribe another individual is to gain an advantage by addressing the greed of the recipient. In some markets, and in some countries this is deemed normal practice, so it comes down to, not only the best product or service specification, but also the most generous bribe. To make something like this 'ethical', if it can be, if all the parties understand the process and play the same game, the process will be fairly conducted. If, however, one party is unaware of the bribery, this will distort the process, and it can then be argued that this would then be highly unethical.

Honesty – This is one of the virtues that people often associate with ethical behaviour, as there is consistency in the approach that an honest party will take, and can therefore be relied upon to take.

Fairness – Like honesty, fairness provide a consistency in the approach the individual or organisation takes to all parties.

Pricing – This relates to providing value for money. If a product or service is over priced and/or under provided, a customer will feel cheated, and the offering deemed unethical. This is not always the case, but is a useful rule of thumb.

Personnel – It is people that make up organisations and their ethics and morals are on the front-line with the customers. When staff act in an ethical and fair way towards customers, the perceived value to the customer is likely to increase.

Advertising – Misleading advertising is an immediate killer of ethical perception as it infers that the whole message is a lie and therefore untrustworthy.

Confidentiality – As part of the trustworthiness of a person, organisation or brand, trustworthiness relies on confidentiality.

Distortion – When facts or truths are distorted, trust can be affected.

These factors follow the new advertising industry ethics code which also quotes five core values:

- Integrity
- Respect
- Fairness
- Trustworthiness
- Professional excellence[xv]

New ethical problems – The rise of the electronic media, and the freedom of workforce movement has lead to new ethical dilemmas, such as the intrusion of privacy, discrimination or the trapping of customers.

Intrusion of privacy – With the advent of fast computer processing and data storage, personal data can be filed and retrieved very quickly. Security is a major issue in modern business life, and failure to secure personal data, or the misuse of it, has led to the notion that our privacy is being invaded, breaking down trust.

Discrimination – The modern, cosmopolitan society in which we now live can have no place for discrimination or bigotry. Individuals and organisations that practice or even just exhibit the traits of discrimination are often seen as unethical and untrustworthy. Discrimination can take the form of racial, gender, religious, ability/disability or intellectual, to name but a few.

Ethical conflicts – Organisations are in existence to make money, and this can often conflict with the views of their staff, board, customers or market as a whole. The conflicts mentioned include conflicts with customers, competitors, society, subordinates, peers, etc.

Relationship marketing philosophy – The basis of every transaction is to start, or maintain a relationship with the customer. This relationship, however, must be built on a foundation of mutual trust and ethical uniformity.

Customer Relationship Management (or sometimes Marketing) or CRM has become big business over the years. These systems try to automate the relationships a company has with its customers, something that comes naturally to a good salesperson. The automation of the relationship causes problems, as no computer can fully replace complex human interaction.

Recent developments in CRM systems mean that we can now collect analyse and use more information about the individual than ever before. Classifications such as the ACORN groupings are becoming irrelevant as computer systems allow us to aggregate customers according to ever changing criteria. This is where we start hitting data privacy issues and Data Protection legislation.

If someone steps onto your property uninvited, they invade your 'personal space'. When a company collects information on you and your interests and activities, and then makes use of it, does this not also invade this space? It may not be a physical invasion, but it builds a picture of you as a customer, but one that may be distorted – the distortion then applies to you throughout that organisation, or, if sold on, within the marketplace.

Think for a moment about one of the most successful websites to employ intelligence to get closer to the customer – the Amazon online bookshop. Based on your purchases in the past, and other people's purchasing patterns of the same products, Amazon attempt to predict other products you would be interested in. In theory, this is a great feature as it encourages increased cross sales, and can prove very informative for the customer.

BUT – What if you buy a one-off present, say a book or toy for the child of an acquaintance, as I have done. In the way Amazon operates, your profile will have this purchase recorded against it and they will always assume that you want to buy children's products. This is, however, an annoyance and not really an intrusion of privacy, but if they sold this distorted view of your behaviour to a third party, it would then raise privacy issues. Amazon does not sell data to anyone else though.

Given the claim that companies lose half their customers every five years[xvi], it is important to build loyalty and therefore trust amongst the customer base. Customer loyalty is built up over time and is non-transferable. It is based on favourable customer experiences, trust and allegiance. The higher the level of customer service offered the higher the degree of customer loyalty.

With the advent of the Internet, CRM has taken on an 'electronic' personality, cultivating and managing multiple relationships online with customers, partners and suppliers, normally in real-time. But it does require fast reactions and accurate profiling, as shown in Sindell's customer valuation feedback model, in Figure 5.

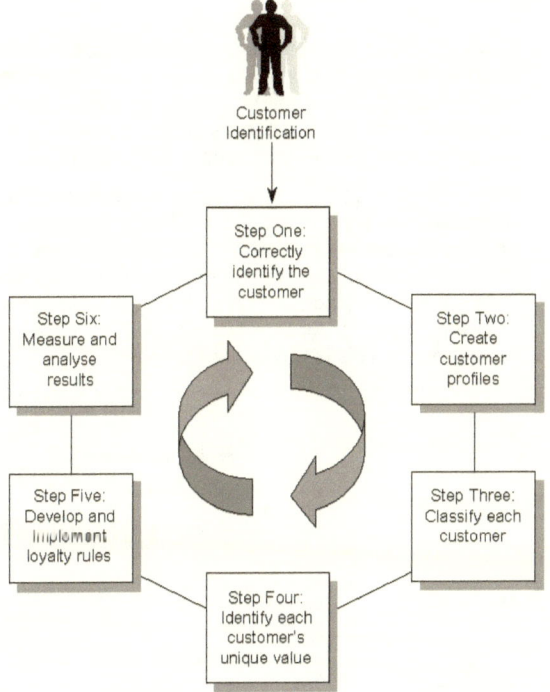

Figure 5. Customer valuation feedback model[xvii]

Sindell's customer valuation feedback model demonstrates the value feedback normally present in an e-CRM package. Whilst the software may undertake this analysis, a lack of understanding amongst the operators can often lead to errors being made and thus damaging the company or brand reputation. The steps are as follows:

1. *Correctly identify the customer.* For many companies this is not an easy task
2. *Profile each customer.* The customer valuation model is used to determine the profile of each customer's potential value
3. *Classify the customer.* Sort customers based on their potential value to your company
4. *Identify what makes each customer different.* Spot what is the unique situation of a customer at any point in time
5. *Define and implement your company's loyalty rules.* Create rules that prescribe the actions to be taken when these unique circumstances have been identified
6. *Measure and analyse the outcomes.* Track customer response to advertising campaigns and special promotions

Data privacy

Privacy is seen as an important ethical issue in many European countries due to past abuses; for example, the Nazi used personal information to persecute the Jews in the 1930's. This perception is not so widely mirrored in countries such as the USA, where freedom of speech and movement are written into the constitution.

Privacy relates to the non-disclosure of any information that is attributable to a single individual. This means that information such as your name, date of birth and address are private, but aggregated data such as knowing you are one of x number of people in a community. Aggregated data includes consumer classification systems, such as socio-economic groups or ACORN (A Classification Of Residential Neighbours). This is highlighted below.

ACORN Category	ACORN groups	ACORN types		CACI 2004 Population Projections	
				Number	%
1 Wealthy achievers	A - Wealthy executives	1.	Wealthy mature professionals, large houses	910,634	1.5
		2.	Wealthy working families with mortgages	787,387	1.3
		3.	Villages with wealthy commuters	1,673,380	2.8
		4.	Well-off manager, larger houses	1,606,739	2.7
	B – Affluent greys	5.	Older affluent professionals	959,555	1.6
		6.	Farming communities	1,142,988	1.9
		7.	Old people, detached homes	1,119,361	1.9
		8.	Mature couples, smaller detached homes	1,193,842	2.0
		9.	Older families, prosperous suburbs	1,316,014	2.2
	C – Flourishing families	10.	Well-off working families with mortgages	1,382,413	2.3
		11.	Well-off managers, detached houses	2,408,494	4.0
		12.	Large families & houses in rural areas	365,121	0.6
2 – Urban prosperity	D – Prosperous professionals	13.	Well-off professionals, larger houses & converted flats	466,419	0.8
		14.	Older professionals in suburban houses & apartments	843,525	1.4
	E – Educated urbanites	15.	Affluent urban professionals, flats	652,963	1.1
		16.	Prosperous young professionals, flats	494,234	0.8
		17.	Young educated workers, flats	329,891	0.6
		18.	Multi-ethnic young, converted flats	667,067	1.1
		19.	Suburban privately renting professionals	561,259	0.9
	F – Aspiring singles	20.	Student flats & cosmopolitan sharers	392,463	0.7
		21.	Singles & sharers, multi-ethnic areas	1,014,727	1.7
		22.	Low income singles, small rented flats	736,861	1.2
		23.	Student terraces	239,451	0.4
3 – Comfortably off	G – Starting out	24.	Young couples, flats & terraces	552,549	0.9
		25.	White collar singles/sharers, terraces	835,095	1.4
	H – Secure families	26.	Younger white-collar couples with mortgages	1,122,479	1.9
		27.	Middle income, home owning areas	2,045,238	3.4
		28.	Working families with mortgages	1,530,952	2.6
		29.	Mature families in suburban semis	1,987,871	3.3
		30.	Established home owning workers	2,284,331	3.8
		31.	Home owning Asian family areas	653,036	1.1
		32.	Retired home owners	512,288	0.9
	I – Settled suburbia	33.	Middle income, older couples	1,765,633	3.0
		34.	Lower incomes, older people, semis	1,262,693	2.1
	J – Prudent pensioners	35.	Elderly singles, purpose built flats	358,854	0.6
		36.	Older people, flats	1,215,048	2.0

ACORN Category	ACORN groups	ACORN types		CACI 2004 Population Projections	
				Number	%
4 – Moderate means	K – Asian communities	37.	Crowded Asian terraces	269,216	0.5
		38.	Low income Asian families	624,518	1.0
	L – Post industrial families	39.	Skilled older families, terraces	1,677,613	2.8
		40.	Young working families	1,170,142	2.0
	M – Blue collar roots	41.	Skilled workers, semis and terraces	2,289,256	3.8
		42.	Home owning families, terraces	1,570,320	2.6
		43.	Older people, rented terraces	1,041,137	1.7
5 – Hard-pressed	N – Struggling families	44.	Low income larger families, semis	2,023,627	3.4
		45.	Low income, older people, smaller semis	1,853,694	3.1
		46.	Low income, routine jobs, terraces & flats	792,960	1.3
		47.	Low income families, terraced estates	1,572,871	2.6
		48.	Families & single parents, semis & terraces	1,278,089	2.1
		49.	Large families & single parents, many children	904,576	1.5
	O – Burdened singles	50.	Single elderly people, council flats	951,337	1.6
		51.	Single parents & pensioners, council terraces	1,061,787	1.8
		52.	Families & single parents, council flats	509,718	0.9
	P – High-rise hardship	53.	Old people, many high-rise flats	385,342	0.6
		54.	Singles & single parents, high-rise estates	492,156	0.8
	Q – Inner city adversity	55.	Multi-ethnic purpose built estates	626,469	1.1
		56.	Multi-ethnic crowded flats	628,975	1.1
	Unclassified			490,427	0.8
	TOTAL			60,005,095	100.0

Table 1. UK consumer classification by ACORN groups[xviii]

Customer privacy concerns were highlighted by Sindell, in her book[xix]:

- *Provide an understandable, easily accessible privacy policy statement.* Prominently display the firm's commitment to privacy, whether the website collects customer information or not
- *Assure customers that privacy policies are binding, even through mergers and acquisitions.* Additionally, assure them that purchasing information will not be sold to third parties, where it can result in unwanted e-mail solicitations, telemarketing calls, or stolen identities
- *Educate consumers about privacy.* Allay vague privacy issues and show consumers where they should focus their online privacy concerns. In other words, help consumers define their privacy fears
- *Promote your e-corporation's privacy policy.* Letting customers know how you protect their privacy will help you build trust and loyalty
- *Over comply with regulations.* Show customers that you are willing to go the extra mile on their behalf. You can serve your customers (and build long-term relationships) by helping them protect their own privacy

In Europe, privacy is protected by law using the Data Protection Act (DPA) (different names exist throughout the EU). This is designed to safeguard the identity and privacy of the European citizen, and avoid the persecution experienced by some of the population in Europe in the last century. Other countries, most notably the USA, whilst having put formal legislation in place early on, believe largely in self-regulation. Whilst the legislative route is no guarantee against the occurrence of abuse, there is more chance within a system self-regulated by the interested parties and backed up by law.

The Data Protection regulations that came into force in Britain in December 2003 shows the direction the EU is taking with their Data Protection Directive. The focus of the act is to enforce an active and positive opt-in amongst consumers. The rule does not implicitly cover business-to-business (B2B) customers, but I would argue that as these customers are individuals too, and if the details are that of a person (direct dial phone line, personalised e-mail address, etc), then it would be good practice, even ethically sound, to treat them as 'individuals'.

The fact that the regulations only officially relate to business-to-consumer (B2C) markets is something many commentators and companies seem to forget (or indeed ignore) – business customers are consumers to other companies. Because of this dual role, business customers will become accustomed to the way they are dealt with as a consumer, and may expect this from business contacts – failure to do it may aggravate the relationship despite being legally sound.

The DPA has altered the face of online marketing, as it has for direct offline marketing and list management in general. The active opt-in required under the DPA has forced many companies to alter their practices. Electronic storage of customer data is also covered, so personal data is protected. Privacy statements, whether on- or offline have all changed to accommodate the changing legislation.

There is a work around for the tight DPA regulations, allowing a company that has sold a product to a customer to communicate 'similar' products or complementary services they offer to the customer, unless they implicitly opt out. This clause will probably need to be tested in a court of law before we understand the full scope of the legislation. This 'soft' opt-in, as it is called, will provide a lifeline to companies during the transition from an unlegislated landscape to a more stringent environment.

Other areas that have been targeted by the regulations include the location-based services (LBS) used on mobile telephones and the use of cookies on websites. LBS technology uses triangulation of telephone masts to pinpoint the mobile phone and to match that to the locality. In this way, a marketer would know that the customer is near their store and, for example, could text them a voucher to encourage them into the outlet – but this still needs the opt-in.

Finally, cookies are bits of Internet code pushed onto a browsing computer by a website to help the site owners recognise returning visitors and record information relevant to the interaction. Cookies improve the customer experience on many websites, but customers must be able to opt-out if necessary without loss of service. If third party cookies are used on the website e.g. by an advertiser, they must also comply fully with the DPA.

2.2 Pan regional/cultural challenges

The ethical issues of international marketing have been of great significance in recent years, as Armstrong, *et al*[xx], point out, owing to publicity and controversy generated from certain international events and legislation occurring in the 1970's and 80's. For example the case of Nestlé's infant formula sales to Third World countries is pertinent. The company has been the subject of an organised boycott within the market, from 1977 to 1984. Nestlé's behaviour initiated a subsequent World Health Organisation (WHO) code on the topic, and the formation of the International Council of Infant Food.

2.2.1 Safe Harbour

Recently the law has also been tightened up in respect to the trade and transfer of personal data. The EU Privacy Directive restricts the transfer of such information to countries outside the Europe, unless they can demonstrate that they adhere to Safe Harbour.

In legal terms, a company must state clearly which legal jurisdiction customers agree to when signing up to the service or buying the product. Part of the international considerations, for example, involves the formation of Safe Harbours; companies that receive or store data about EU citizens have to abide by strict legal and operational guidelines.

Safe Harbour comprises seven key principles:

Notice – companies are required to clearly disclose what information they are collecting, the methods they use to gather it, the purpose of the data, and how the data will be used.

Choice – companies must give consumers the opportunity to refuse the use of their personal data for purposes other than the intended one. Customers could also refuse to have their personal information disclosed to a third party.

Onward Transfer – if a company discloses private information to another party (with consent, of course), that party must also conform to Safe Harbour principles.

Access – companies must give consumers the right to review their personal information to make corrections and deletions

Security – companies are required to take all necessary steps to protect their customers' personal information.

Data Integrity – companies should only collect information that is relevant to the intended purpose.

Enforcement – companies must establish policies to investigate consumer complaints and resolve disputes regarding privacy laws. Companies also must correct any problems that arise from violating Safe Harbour principles.

This legislation is primarily for the US market, but as many US companies point out, infringements in Europe are not being punished, so why should they spend the money and effort to comply with these rules. A study conducted by Arthur Andersen in 2001 highlighted the extent of this problem, in that only two out of seventy-five US companies passed the seven principles[xxi]. Given this apparent rejection of legislation, it is confusing that US consumers identify privacy as their primary concern. A Harris study in 2003 found that 74% of American Internet users said that they wanted spamming outlawed. '.Net' magazine in the UK asked – 'what on earth is wrong with the other 26%?[xxii]?

The distrust American consumers now have to digital marketing practices is demonstrated by the huge numbers of consumers who opted in to the new Telephone Preference Service (TPS), which, like the European service, allows consumers to indicate their wishes not to be contacted for telesales or telemarketing purposes. Digital marketing must, and is, changing in the US in the face of consumer protest and power.

The legal standpoint in the US provides the marketing industry with the power to dictate the rules as they apply to data privacy. This is because of the American Constitution, the first and fourth, which protect the citizen's right to freedom of speech.

2.2.2 International culture

Modern trade is now global, and the Internet in particular has broken down national boundaries. In most cases, anyone anywhere can register domain names for any country, thus removing the national identity of many brands and companies.

Traditional 'bricks and mortar' companies regularly export physical products around the world, and virtual companies are no different. International trade has never been easier.

The cheap but highly-educated and literate labour found on the Indian subcontinent has led a number of companies to relocate their call centre activities to the region, and with it, the personal records of their customers. It is unclear how legal this transfer is, but the business benefits are well documented. Only Russia and China have, to date, not signed up to prevent spamming activity, and most unsolicited messages appear to originate from these countries[xxiii].

When planning international trade, and/or using the cheaper labour opportunities offered by and the markets, a business must assess the risks of data loss or theft, and most importantly, the impact it would have on customer perception.

The differences in national approach to the issues of data privacy and therefore the perceived ethical use of data relates to historic factors. In Europe, the excesses of the Fascist governments of the 1930's and 40's, and the Communist regimes in the East, have blighted the view of data collection. The unethical purposes to which personal data was used by Stalin and the Nazis have caused the public to distrust information gatherers, especially by governments.

In the USA however, the founding fathers decided that as a response to the oppression of British rule, they would protect the right to free speech. This is now the major stumbling block to legislating unsolicited e-mail messages, as the US Constitution prohibits restricting communications. They have, however, passed laws to limit spam, but commentators are forecasting this to fail, as there is no legal precedent to oppose the Constitution.

The Internet is a global, unregulated network, and no single government appears able or willing to try to regulate it for all users. The French government successfully banned the sale of Nazi memorabilia on the Yahoo! auction site to French nationals, although it does not have any jurisdiction over citizens of other countries.

The UK has a large number of legislative safeguards for personal information, fewer than before as the new data protection legislation has merged many regulations. One that has yet to be included is the TPS, which is a list of telephone numbers that should not be used for telesales purposes. This service has recently been introduced in the USA and 'surprised' the regulators by the high levels of take up – obviously cold calling is a problem in the States.

The legal framework in each country is a factor in shaping the ethical environment of a nation. The ethical way to approach legislation is to adhere to the strictest restrictions that apply to your business, and apply that to all markets.

The ethical frameworks of other countries and regions have developed in a similar way to the UK, with specific regional or national overtones. The following is a comical example of the different international business perspectives.

Whether you trade in a single region, within a single country (with or without regional differences) or internationally, you will confront a variety of ethics specific to the local culture. Abuse them, and you will face the wrath of your customers, possibly even across borders.

Ethics and ethical behaviour differ from country to country, but any business wishing to trade with customers, be they business or consumers, must adhere to most stringent rules in order to demonstrate trustworthiness, and to ensure legal practice.

2.3   What are the ethics/morals

Aristotle is accredited with introducing the element of ethics in communications in his Rhetorica.

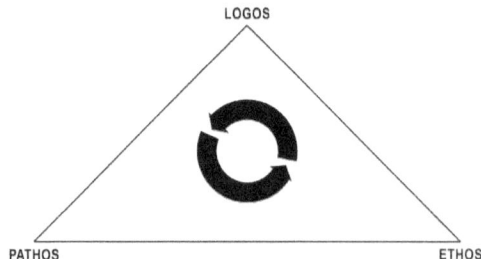

Figure 6. Aristotle's Rhetorica[xxv]

In Aristotle's model, Logos is the word or idea, Pathos is the feeling or emotion and Ethos, the origin of the word ethic is the character or ethics of the communication. If any element is missing, this will lead to an unethical communication, which in this model cannot exist, and is therefore not a true communication – a propaganda if you like.

Philosophers today usually divide ethical theories into three general subject areas: metaethics, normative ethics, and applied ethics. *Metaethics* investigates where our ethical principles come from, and what they mean. Are they merely social inventions? Do they involve more than expressions of our individual emotions? Metaethical answers to these questions focus on the issues of universal truths, the will of God, the role of reason in ethical judgments, and the meaning of ethical terms themselves. *Normative ethics* takes on a more practical task, which is to arrive at moral standards that regulate right and wrong conduct. This may involve articulating the good habits that we should acquire, the duties that we should follow, or the consequences of our behaviour on others. Finally, *applied ethics* involves examining specific controversial issues, such as abortion, infanticide, animal rights, environmental concerns, homosexuality, capital punishment, or nuclear war. By using the conceptual tools of metaethics and normative ethics, discussions in applied ethics try to resolve these controversial issues. The lines of distinction between metaethics, normative ethics, and applied ethics are often blurry[xxvi].

Ethics are essentially about the rights and wrongs of a situation or approach. It is not easy to define exactly what is right or wrong though as other factors influence the ethics. Culture is probably the most prominent factor within a society.

Society itself is becoming almost obsessed by the question of ethics in relation to businesses, especially online where the speed of unethical practice worries the market with the 'hit-and-run' tactics employed by a minority. However, compliance to the local ethical standards need not be an onerous task for companies.

Baker highlighted the stakeholders that might be affected by or influence the ethics of an organisation[xxvii]:

- Customers
- Employees
- Local communities
- Government
- Intermediaries
- Suppliers
- The financial community

It could be argued that unethical practices would attract a wider audience, including the religious community. Conversely, blatantly ethical practices could attract others (albeit within the communities listed) such as the Co-operative bank in the UK that prides itself in its ethical investments.

The Laczniak and Murphy prototypical normative model[xxviii] applies the following questions to the evaluation of the ethics of marketing practices:

i) Does the contemplated action violate the law? (legal test)

ii) Is this action contrary to widely accepted moral obligations? (duties test)

iii) Does the proposed action violate any other special obligations that stem from the type of marketing organisation at focus? (special obligations test)

iv) Is the intent of the contemplated action harmful? (motives test)

v) Is it likely that any major damages to people or organisations will result from the contemplated action? (consequences test)

vi) Is there a satisfactory alternative action that produces equal or greater benefits to the parties affected than the proposed action? (utilitarian test)

vii) Does the contemplated action infringe upon property rights, privacy rights, or the inalienable rights of the consumer? (rights test)

viii) Does the proposed action leave another person or group less well off? Is this person or group already a member of a relatively underprivileged class? (justice test)

If a marketer answers yes to any of these questions, the decision is probably unethical and should be reconsidered.

In addition to the ethical standards set by the local or national moral codes, a company adopting so-called 'green' policies can often be seen as adopting an ethical approach – examples would include The Body Shop, who promote their ecological credentials, but it could be argued that this philosophy is an ethical approach, although the company do not push that aspect.

Many US companies are falling foul of their national Government's approach to the Green issues. The petrol company Exxon-Mobil (famous for the Esso brand) have a hard enough time as a 'polluting' supplier, but they are also accused of sponsoring President George Bush and many Senators, ensuring their continued opposition to the Kyoto agreement and anti-pollution lobbies – this is seen as highly unethical, and the company is often boycotted in Europe.

Country ethics and morals

The ethics of a country are often set and controlled by the Government, either in terms of legislation, or more subtlety in terms of education. Again, looking at the German experience pre-war, when the Nazi Government educated a generation of school children with their politics that ended in the blind faith of many of the young boys dying in a desperate rear-guard action to save the war in 1944.

Regional ethics and morals

Regions can either be within a country or span a number of countries. Within a country, the division can either be as a result of geographic location, or in terms of ethics, in religious groupings – for example the divisions of India following independence into two other states, both of which are Muslim as opposed India's Hindu majority. Obviously, the Indian example is one of a very large country. In other countries, religious, linguistic or cultural differences can cause divisions, and therefore, in some cases differences in the moral and ethical outlook of the people.

3.   Trust

3.1   Trusting environments

Trust is defined as a firm reliance on the integrity, ability or character of a person, company or thing[xxix].

We live in a world where people are sceptical about every claim anyone makes. In some cases rightly so, especially when you see how many fraudsters, criminals and other undesirables are trying to deceive the public. This means that any claim that is made should be backed up in some credible way.

The only real way to prove ethical behaviour is to demonstrate it through actions. Consistent ethical business practices and marketing campaigns will, over time, show customers the sincerity of a company's intentions.

Trust is the foundation of all customer loyalty, satisfaction and relationships. But, customer trust is not the only element. Figure 5 shows the influence of trust throughout the organisation, and the fact that it offers a virtuous circle of opportunities for the organisation.

One of the major factors in business is 'Trust'. The belief that you are operating ethically involves an element of trust from the customers. This trust extends beyond the brand name, or product to the company as a whole, including customer-facing employees, such as sales people, customer care telephone operators, etc. I have spent most of my marketing career in the 'back office', but always find myself talking to people who, upon learning the name of my employer (irrespective of the employer at the time), always seem to have an experience to relay to me – good or bad – I am instantly a customer-facing employee.

The cornerstone of business

Trust is the cornerstone of profitable business as it strengthens relationships. The comment from my former boss about people buying from their friends backs this up. You will generally find that ethics are a major factor in the building and maintaining of trustworthiness, and should permeate throughout the company.

The bottom line for marketers is one of trust. Senia cites that "Trust means having the customer comfortable with handing over personal information and engaging in ongoing commercial transactions at a company's website[xxx]." Trust has always been a key element in successful marketing. In industrial marketing, the 20% of the sales force that sells 80% of the volume owes much of its success to building trust-based relationships with clients[xxxi].

Trust is defined as "the belief that a party's word or promise is reliable and a party will fulfil his/her obligations in an exchange relationship[xxxii]. Trust is at the core of most relationships between human beings. We all have a sense of what it means to trust someone. The parameters of trust are often personal, and thus, decentralisation is the nature of trust, because each individual has his/her own opinions[xxxiii]. But as Matt Ridley pointed out, 'Our minds have been built by selfish genes, but they have been built to be social, trustworthy and co-operative[xxxiv].'

This trust, however, is a two way process, as indicated by the phrase 'exchange relationship', and the company must be confident that the information given by the customer is accurate so that any targeted marketing is itself accurate, otherwise there may be a claim that the data collection is incorrect and they are being inundated with junk mail or 'spam.[xxxv].'

When the seller is allowed to know some personal data about a customer's preferences, a trust relationship is implied[xxxvi]. It comes down to a company building and maintaining a feeling of trust and confidence with its customers[xxxvii].

Barber[xxxviii] said that trust implies expectations of the future, which can be broken down into three forms of expectations:
1. Expectation to fulfil moral orders
2. Expectation to perform roles competently
3. Expectation that fiduciary obligations will be met

So Abdul-Rahman lists the properties of trust as follow:[xxxix]
- Trust is subjective
- Trust is situation specific
- Trust is agent specific
- Trust is not absolute; it exists as levels of trust
- Trust involves expectations of future outcome
- Situations of trust can result in positive or negative outcomes, thus involves risk, uncertainty and ignorance
- Trust gives control to the trustee and an opportunity to betray the truster
- Trust delays monitoring of trustee's actions until after choice of action is made
- Trustees are active agents that have the ability to perform with a degree of independence from the truster's control
- Trust is not prediction
- Trust is not transitive

Children are taught to be trustworthy with the following points:
- **Be honest** - Don't lie, cheat, or steal
- **Be reliable** - Keep your promises and follow through on your commitments
- **Have the courage** - To do what is right, even when it is difficult
- **Be a good friend** - and don't betray a trust

John McKean identified the primary needs of customers in his book – Customer Are People[xl]:

- **_Acknowledgement_**
  Acknowledge the customer and their importance

- **_Respect_**
  Respect the customer and their needs

- **_Trust_**
  Build trust in the customer so they feel like buying your product is the best decision for them

McKean goes on to develop his 'Leader's Promise to Employees'. I would argue that this is a promise that can also be used to relate to customers too.

I'll ACKNOWLEDGE you – recognise your worth
I'll be ACCOMMODATING – change things for your needs
I'll be ACCOUNTABLE – take ownership of my decisions and their outcome
I'll be COMMUNICATIVE – openly exchange ideas/information with you
I'll be CONSIDERATE – think of you first
I'll be COURAGEOUS – bold and tenacious, even when it's tough
I'll be EMPATHETIC – sensitive to your feelings
I'll be ETHICAL – do what is right
I'll be FAIR – balance your needs with others
I'll be FLEXIBLE – balance your needs with others
I'll be GENEROUS – give more than expected
I'll be HONEST – tell the truth
I'll have HUMILITY – give credit and avoid self-importance
I'll be INSPIRING – provide enthusiasm toward a goal
I'll be LOYAL – always there for you
I'll be PERSONABLE – easy to deal with
I'll be RESPECTFUL – recognise your dignity as a person
I'll be SUPPORTIVE – provide help and remove barriers
I'll be TOLERANT – accept you without judgment and forgive mistakes
I'll be TRUSTING – believe in you
I'll be TRUSTWORTHY – do what I say and what needs to be done

McKean's Leader's Promise to Employees[xli]

Trust has always been a key element in successful marketing. In industrial marketing, the 20% of the sales force that sells 80% of the volume owes much of its success to building trust-based relationships with clients. To preserve trust and confidence in the relationship, a smart salesperson will even recommend a competitor's product if it better serves the customer's needs[xlii].

This focus on trustworthiness is also a factor in Michael Porter's model of competitive advantage (see Figure 7). In most markets an element of trust must be present in order to encourage long-term customer relationships. This in turn, if properly cultivated can turn in to a competitive advantage, especially in international markets where ethical views differ, sometimes widely. In a trust-based approach, companies rely on the reputation of their existing product to reach customers in e-commerce[xliii]. Winning the customers' trust and keeping their trust, is essential to e-business[xliv].

The key to continue building the trust already garnered through branding efforts. If we don't behave ethically on our own when using customers' names and demographic information, the customers will see to it that legislation, business watchdog groups and privacy organisation force us to do so[xlv].

Competitive Advantage

		Lower Costs	Differentiation
Competitive Scope	Broad Target	Cost Leadership	Differentiation
	Narrow Target	Cost Focus	Focused Differentiation

Figure 7. Porter's generic strategies & competitive advantage

According to Carrigan *et al.* there are a number of reasons why consumers show a distinct lack of ethical awareness when it comes to purchasing goods or services[xlvi]:

- Lack of information - although many respondents in the Dragon International study felt that they did not have enough data to make such ethical purchasing decisions, those who did have company knowledge professed that they did not necessarily act upon it

- No pressure for companies to become "actively ethical" - whilst consumers often punish unethical companies they do not necessarily reward ethical organisations. Many people believe that businesses have a responsibility not to do harm (e.g. use slave labour or produce dangerous by-products during manufacturing) but that they do not automatically have an obligation to help others (e.g. sponsor a local community project)
- Gap between attitude and behaviour found that although consumers had socially responsible attitudes, only 20 percent had actually acted upon these views and purchased something in the last year because the product was associated with a good cause[xlvii]
- Lack of personal impact - if an organisation's behaviour has no direct impact on an individual, they are unlikely to take any action. "Ethics" tends to be viewed in generalist terms and relatively few consumers are aware of specific company cases

Taking the direct approach with honesty builds trust. McKean, quotes from the 'Little Yellow Book' which says, "Test the ethics of contemplated action by asking the question, *'Would I want to see it in the headlines tomorrow morning?'*" This is the TV test again[xlviii].

So, on what bases should the customer trust the marketer? Ali and Birley explored the role of trust, and used the following diagram to explain their findings[xlix]:

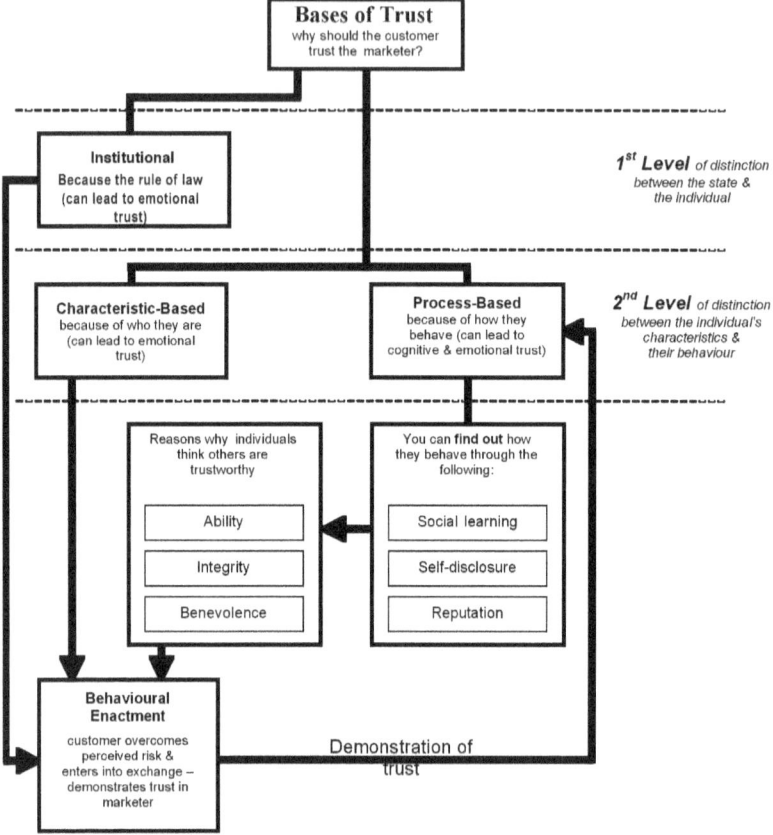

Figure 8. Role of trust[I]

The trust elements from Ali and Birley's model (Figure 8) are as follows:

Characteristic based trust

This only relates to individuals; it cannot be acquired in the way that the other two forms of trust can be obtained. Its presence or absence is a cognitive factor between the focal individual and the third party, and exists if the third party feels that there is a social similarity between themselves and the focus individual.

Ali and Birley noted that characteristic-based trust is a commodity, which exists according to the inherent characteristics of an individual and their perception by the wider social environment.

Process based trust

The association between trust and long-term relationships (process-based trust) is well documented and emphasises that exchanges required trust will not be a historical instances, namely they will not take place on a one-off basis.

Social exchange theory also shows the association between trust and long-term exchange.

The research from Ali and Birley demonstrates that the amount of risk someone is willing to take in another person depends on how much they trust them.

Much has been written in recent months about the Data Protection legislation that was tightened throughout Europe in late 2003. Europe now has amongst the strictest legislation in the world, and it makes commercial sense for any company operating internationally, to adopt the strictest rules thus exceeding many consumers perception and setting new standards.

Consumers will enter into a trusting and enduring relationship with suppliers on the basis of the exchange of information. This quote comes from Urban, *et al.* who express the opinion that trust will soon become the currency of the Internet[li].

The concept of trust is wide-ranging, and has been considered in a variety of different environments, but arguably was first studied in the context of psychology and sociology. Sociologists are able to say that "without trust, society would not be possible, trust increases order by reducing complexity… to examine each interaction for its potential negative consequences would paralyse the social actor; thus, trust orders society[lii].'

Brad Lich, the VP Marketing of e-Chemicals stated, "we have believed since our inception that building a trusted brand is essential to our success[liii]." Ali and Birley identified a model, which addresses these issues of trust issues[liv]:

- On what bases should customer trust the marketer? We distinguish between the entrepreneurs' characteristics; the rule of law and how they behave
- Specifically, in terms of the latter, we then consider how customers find out whether the marketer is trustworthy. This is maybe through a combination of social learning, self-disclosure or reputation
- Why do others consider entrepreneurs to be trustworthy (based on behaviour)? The answer is because of the possible combination of antecedents to trust specifically, ability, integrity and benevolence

Unfortunately, the online consumer, with the very short attention spans Jakob Nielsen highlights, may lose trust in online activities not only in dealing with a single company, but through poor service or illegal practices of other companies, even competitors.

The 'bases of trust' approach explains trust may exist due to the rule of law or shared personal characteristics. The 'forms of trust' approach shares some common ground with the above, but the essential difference appears to be that it allows for the existence of 'affect-based trust' (i.e. people may trust each other because of emotional bonds). The 'antecedent factors' approach appears to be the most holistic since it seeks to identify specific antecedent factors that may account for the existence of trust between two people[iv]. This therefore demonstrates that trust relationships are complex, multi-layered functions that require careful planning and maintenance, especially if there is a commercial element to that relationship.

Some commentators have attempted to quantify the elements of trust, with hugely complex formulae, which, not being a mathematician, I find difficult to apply to the real world, but the concept is relevant. Chen and Yeager say trust becomes a social contract with social implications for the participants. They have developed a formula for evaluating the value of trust.

The above sub-section gives us an overview of how the two components of trust relationships, Confidence and Risk, map to hard coded information. This sub-section will discuss how to propagate such information to make a complex chain of relationships.

The following is a simple algorithm to rate a propagated "degree of trust." Here, a peer can have a trust value of −1, 0, 1, 2, 3, or 4 [3]:

Value	Meaning
-1	Distrust
0	Ignore
1	Minimal trust
2	Average trust
3	Good trust
4	Complete trust

Table 2. Trust value

For the trust values of 0 and −1, the associated codat is never accessed. The trust value will be propagated through a transaction pipe. The trust value of a target for a single path, $\mathrm{Vpath(T)}$, from peer S to peer T through peers Pi, $\mathrm{I= 1, 2, ..., n}$, can be calculated as follows:

W here V(Pi) is greater than or equal to 1,

$$V_{path}(T) = \frac{1}{4n}(\sum_{i=1}^{n} V(P_j)) \times V(T)$$

Formula 1

Here, $V(Pi)$ is the trust value of the peer, Pi, who provides the information. $V(T)$ is the trust value on the target peer, T.

This is the only reference to empirical trust evaluation, Chen and Yeager's work is available for those who want to pursue it. A simpler format is demonstrated by Abdul-Rahman and Hailes[lvi], in which they use personalities to convey the point.

(Alice trusts Bob) & (Bob trusts Cathy)

= Alice trusts Cathy

This is not *generally* true. We posit that transitivity may hold if certain conditions are met. We have termed this *conditional transitivity* and the conditions that may allow transitivity are (with reference to the example above):

a) Bob explicitly communicates his trust in Cathy to Alice, as a 'recommendation'
b) Alice trusts Bob as a recommender, i.e. recommender trust exists in the system
c) Alice is allowed to make judgements about the 'quality' of Bob's recommendation (based on Alice's policies)
d) Trust is not absolute, i.e. Alice may trust Cathy less than Bob does, based on Bob's recommendation

This indicates that trust is transferable, which many commentators, including Adul-Rahman and Hailes, refuse to acknowledge, indeed Luhmann states, *"[Trust] is not transferable to other objects or to people who trust[lvii]."* In some senses this is correct, but in research carried out with online customers, 'recommendation from a friend' is the most common reason for registration on a website.

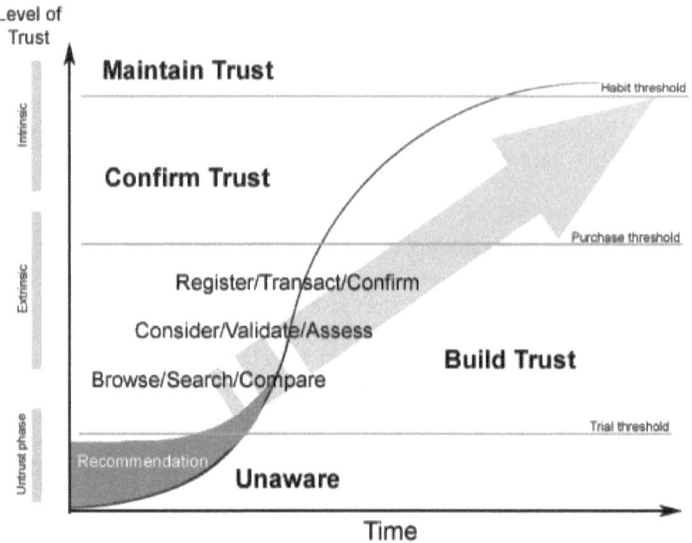

Figure 9. The trust lifecycle[lviii]

Whilst complete, unerring trust is not transferable, Figure 9 attempts to demonstrate trust, in terms of confidence in the supplier. The recommendation implies a more trusting start to a new relationship, dependent on the trust in the referrer. This 'recommendation' can be seen in the dark area in the graph, signifying the level of trust in the referrer. In normal circumstances first contacts with a supplier will be cautious, whereas, if the contact has been initiated through a recommendation, the customer starts with a greater level of confidence, and therefore trust.

Abdul-Rahman quoted Bailey who said, *"[trust] is accepted vulnerability to another's possible but not expected ill will (or lack of goodwill) towards one."* This is transposed in saying that when we trust, we accept this risk, but we learn, after the course of action has been taken, whether our trust was warranted by the results of this trusting behaviour[lix], shown in the graph in diagram 9 as the huge slope still to climb in the trusting relationship, even after the recommendation from the friend or colleague.

The transferred trust is a valuable commodity, and is one that organisations such as Linked-in (**www.linkedin.com**) and eCademy (**www.ecademy.co.uk**) see as almost having a trading value. A recommendation does not infer complete, irreversible trust, but it does provide a short cut from an untrusted phase to a more trusting relationship.

The confidence factor mentioned in relation to the graph in Figure 10 has been defined by Misztal as follows[ix]:

> *The main difference between trust and confidence is connected with the degree of certainty that we attach to our expectations. It is, of course, much easier to decide whether to have confidence or not in one's milkman than to decide which people can be trusted to reciprocate friendly actions, since trust involves a difficult task of assessment of other people's capacities for the action.*

Figure 10. Trust and confidence cycle[lxi]

3.1.1 Customers

Spreeman's asymmetric information flow shown in Figure 11, is a newly published model for the financial markets, and demonstrates the principle shown in Figure 9 and Figure 10, in that the initial contact can only build the company profile in the marketplace, beginning the relationship with the customer. The second step builds the brand image within that marketplace to allow contact with the customer to advise and interact with them (remember this is a model for the financial markets).

Finally, the after-sales and retention will build the brand reputation, reputation is something that is enhanced by trust, and customers who have reached this step will help build this reputation by recommending the brand/company to friends and acquaintances.

Figure 11. The asymmetric information flow model[lxii]

Information can take on a life of its own, and may be used outside the purpose for which it was originally conveyed. That is no longer an ethical concern, it is a legal one, and businesses cannot afford to ignore it and pretend that the privacy debate will disappear[lxiii].

A proactive approach to dealing with issues of consumer privacy would involve four major issues:

- Maintaining an ongoing dialogue with consumers
- Educating consumers and promoting privacy efforts
- Creating an industry standard for addressing the privacy issue
- Continuing to lobby for and against government regulation[lxiv]

Most websites do not focus on building trust as part of an ongoing relationship with customers. Most companies with 'hard-sell' sites generally fail in their marketing approach, primarily because they fail to address trust issues, as shown in the following table[lxv].

Trust dimension	The Strategy Spectrum		
	High-Pressure Selling	Trust Building	Trusting Relationship
Sales Approach	Get the business. Close the sale	Honest matching to customer needs. Consultative sales	Build relationships to become the advocate of the customer's interests
Products	Offer manufacturer's products only. Sell highest margin products	Manufacturer's products with links to competitors' website	All products available via links to competitors' sites
Information	Slanted toward the manufacturer. Biased view of competing products	Unbiased view of manufacturer's complete range of products	Unbiased view of all competing products and services. Credible advice
Advertising	Flashing banners on a cluttered website. Hard selling, 'buy now' approach	Although adverts are presented, the customer is given the option to omit them	Adverts are available on demand, but control is in the hands of the customer
Price	Low prices, off-price promotions, deal-making orientation	Honest, value-based offerings	Offers value-added features and services at a premium price
Service	Minimal service and support	Guarantees to ensure customer satisfaction	Ensure the customer receives all the benefits promised over the full life of the product
Time Frame	Short-term view, transaction-orientated with high customer churn	Intermediate time frame with focus on delivering extra value to the customer	Long-term approach that wins and retains customers, increasing account penetration

Table 3. Choosing between high pressure sales & complete trust[lxvi]

The model shown in Table 3 highlights the different strategic (and in some cases tactical) actions through different [trust] dimensions leading from high-pressure sales, through trust building to a trusting relationship. It is important that marketers understand that the trusting relationship should be the goal.

Brand trust is a major driver in Europe's adoption of e-commerce in which shoppers' familiarity with the channel and the overall process of buying online is a key factor. The countries in which consumers are familiar with using credits cards are leading the way within Europe[lxvii], demonstrating the far-reaching impact of this trust. This trust extends across on- and offline markets.

> Whoever has more influence over the control and evolution of this [Internet] technology will ultimately be able to leverage this market power to their advantage. This could be online consumers. It could be online businesses. It may be specific industries. It could even be governments. A carefully thought out strategic reaction to the consumer privacy issue is absolutely critical for private industry and, ultimately, to the evolution of e-commerce[lxviii].

The quote from Prabhaker shows that trust relationships can be used as a competitive advantage, as discussed earlier. These relationships are, however, very complex whether they involve private or public sectors, or both, as cited by Prabhaker.

Companies, as has been stated, have spent millions launching CRM platforms to build relationships with customers, but forget to then build a trustworthy image with those customers. It is difficult to decide which element should precede the other – should a company build a trustworthy image before building a relationship, or will the relationship build trust?

In a report from the World Economic Forum, researched showed that citizens have as much trust in the media and in trade unions as they have in their national (mostly elected) governments. It also showed that trust in executives of domestic companies has fallen more than trust in executives of multi-national companies in most countries[lxix].

Jevons and Gabbott state that trust operates as an 'order qualifier', not and 'order winner[lxx].'" In other words, trust, like product quality, must be at a satisfactory level to even be included in a purchaser's consideration set – the hygiene factors in Figure 8.

The answer lies in the existing image – many companies attempting this would already have a relationship with a marketplace, and a certain image, in which case, the image should be bolstered whilst keeping the existing relationship. For brand new start-ups, both should be developed together as it is unlikely that you would have the luxury of building an image without fostering relationships with customers and keeping the cash flow healthy to run the business.

Nakra suggests a four-tiered approach for marketers, as shown in Table 4.

Level	Visitors' behaviour	Recommendations for marketers
One	Visitors choose anonymity; they deliberately forgo additional benefits offered by personalisation and premium content.	Build trust by promising not to collect data or use cookies. Eleven million households will be shopping online for the first time in 2000; it will become critical for merchants to build customer trust and loyalty. Advertise privacy policies boldly and in plain English. Make 'opt-out' a standard feature on sites.
Two	Visitors seek targeted content and additional site access. They are not yet ready for two-way communications. They are in "Don't call me, we'll call you" mode of the relationship.	Merchants must promise not to initiate contact with shoppers or disseminate personal information to third parties. Promote privacy policies to move the visitors to the next level of trust. Remind them of the 'opt-out' option.
Three	Consumers are agreeable to two-way communication. Visitors are willing to share more personally identifying information in exchange for proactive notification of specials from marketers.	Personalise communications messages, tailor product solutions to suit individual buyers' behaviour and needs, offer service ad support. Take advantage of opportunity to communicate via traditional and electronic media. Reinforce privacy policies; 'Keep "opt-out options" as permanent feature of the site. Assure information safety and security.
Four	A trusting relationship has developed by this stage. Customers seek advice and solicitation from marketer at this stage, including deals from established partners.	Create a culture to monitor and secure the information collected. Keep data clean and allow the visitors to audit, correct or request removal of undesirable (from their perspective) information. Use technology and commonsense to guard against information seepage.

Table 4. The four-tier privacy model[lxxi]

McKnight and Chervany claimed that trust was formed of a series of interrelated constructs, as demonstrated in Figure 12[lxxii].

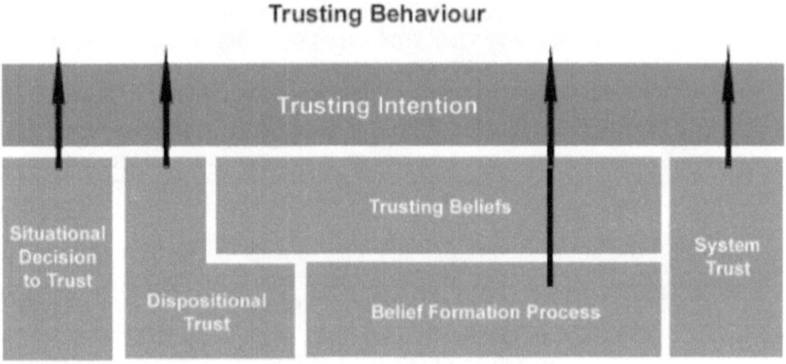

Trusting Behaviour

Figure 12. Trust constructs

In Figure 12, McKnight and Chervany try to indicate the constructs of trust, using arrows to show relationships. Constructs crossed by the arrows are those that mediate the relationship.

They classify the relationships as follows:

"... beliefs/attitudes (in this case Trusting Beliefs) lead to intentions (Trusting Intention), which, in turn, readily becomes manifest in behaviours (Trusting Behaviour). The logic here is simple. When one has Trusting Beliefs about another, one will be willing to depend on that person (Trusting Intention). If one intends to depend on the person, then one will behave in ways to manifest that intention to depend (Trusting Behaviour).

The definitions for Figure 12 are as follows. *Trusting Intention* is defined as "the extent to which one party is willing to depend on the other party in a given situation with a feeling of relative security, even though negative consequences are possible.

Trusting Behaviour indicates the act of trusting, based on Trusting Intentions. *Trusting Beliefs* in the truster's belief in the level of the trustee's trustworthiness as well as the truster's own confidence in that belief.

Situational Decision to Trust is the truster's willingness to trust for a given situation, regardless of the entities involved. *System Trust* has gained importance in modern social relationships over the more spontaneous interpersonal trust, not that it is easy to separate them.

Dispositional Trust is sometimes referred to as 'basic trust' and describes the general trusting attitude of the truster. It is also said that this is a major factor in who we are and is deeply rooted in childhood experiences. It is also cross-situational[lxxiii].

'Spam' e-mail campaigns betray the trust of the consumer. The critical element in relationship marketing – trust – is not just missing here, it has been betrayed[lxxiv]. Technology is not a significant factor in deploying questionable marketing campaigns, but the deliberate deception and misleading aspects of the campaign would have most marketing and business professionals challenging its legitimacy[lxxv].

Research has shown that corporate ethics is an important organisational issue as well as a societal one, and that there is a strong link between corporate ethics and organisational commitment[lxxvi].

The organisation's ethical profile reflects its internal and external public and how it wishes to interact with them: the community, staff, stockholders, and competition.[lxxvii] An IMG Strategies study reported "having basic permission policies (i.e. 'opt-in' policy) is becoming just the price of entry for marketers as opposed the differentiator it used to be[lxxviii]." The price of entry into a market is one of the critical factors here and if 'opt-in' is too high a price, and punishments are severe enough, company ethics will adjust accordingly, and 'spammers' will find new opportunities.

If a customer 'opts in', who decides the use of the personal information, where it is sold and who it is sold to? If it is done right, both the consumer and the marketer can decide, based on the privacy policy. Deciding whom to trust depends on the customer's preferences and the genre of services and products they are interested in buying[lxxix]. Kappelman suggested a list of practices to keep out of e-privacy trouble[lxxx]:

- **Tell it like it is**: Openly disclose your privacy policies
- **Show me**: Let consumers see and correct personal data, just as credit bureaux do
- **Give me a choice**: Let your customers easily 'opt-in' or 'opt-out'
- **Practice quality**: Poor software quality practices cause the security and privacy problems that cost precious customer confidence
- **Stay informed**: Link to good sources of privacy information – be proactive

Privacy and security technology experts agree, according to Mack, that electronic business will suffer setbacks until businesses and consumers have the confidence that the transactions they conduct online will keep their information private and then secure it. Privacy and customer permission has become the cornerstone to customer trust[lxxxi].

A few years ago, it was said that 'The Internet changes everything.' The same could now be said about web trust. The Internet puts such power in the hands of consumers that a new term is needed to describe the paradigm shift: a 'consumer-to-business' (C2B) marketing relationship. They will demand and receive trust-based relationships with preferred vendors. Trust will be the key to survival in this C2B marketing future.[lxxxii]

Finally, we have seen that trust is not a single feeling, or motivation, but can be the sum of a number of drivers and constructs. Barber[lxxxiii] identified a list of circumstances that can also affect or motivate a customer's decision to trust – they may well be negative motivators:

Trust as despair – or choosing from the lesser of two (or more) evils

Trust as social conformity – trust is expected in certain social situations

Trust as innocence – perhaps there was a lack of appreciation of the risks involved

Trust as impulsiveness – acting 'in terms of here and now' instead of pondering on the future outcome

Trust as virtue – when trust is looked upon as a virtue

Trust as masochism – a preference of pain over pleasure, perhaps

Trust as faith – faith in God's help, or whatever turns out is fated. This is called 'extreme trust' but Barber, and probably links to the origins of ethical thinking discussed in an earlier chapter

3.1.1.1 Reader's Digest survey

The Reader's Digest undertakes an annual survey to find the most trusted brands throughout Europe. In the UK, this survey has produced the following results.

Category	2001	2002	2003	2004	2005	2006	2007
Car	Ford	Ford	Ford	Ford	Ford	Ford	Ford
Camera	Canon	Canon	Canon	Canon	Canon	Canon	Canon
Kitchen appliance	Hotpoint	Hotpoint	Hotpoint	Hotpoint	Hotpoint	Hotpoint	Hotpoint
Personal computers	Hewlett Packard	Dell	Dell	Dell	Dell	Dell	Dell
Mobile phone handset	Nokia	Nokia	Nokia	Nokia	Nokia	Nokia	Nokia
Mobile phone service provider	-	-	-	-	-	Orange	O2
Internet Service Providers	AOL	AOL	AOL	AOL	AOL	AOL	BT
Holiday company/tour operator	Thomson	Thomson	Thomson	Thomson	Thomson	Thomson	Thomson
Petrol retailer	-	Esso	Esso	Tesco	Tesco	Tesco	Tesco
Bank/building society	Lloyds TSB	Lloyds TSB	Lloyds TSB	Lloyds TSB	Lloyds TSB	Lloyds TSB	Lloyds TSB
Credit card	-	Visa	Visa	Barclay card	Barclay card	Visa	Visa
Insurance company	-	Prudential	Prudential	Norwich Union	Norwich Union	Norwich Union	Norwich Union
Vitamins	Seven Seas	Seven Seas	Seven Seas	Seven Seas	Seven Seas	Seven Seas	Boots
Cough/cold remedy	Beechams	Beechams	Lemsip	Benylin	Beechams	Beechams	Beechams
Analgesic/pain relief	Nurofen	Nurofen	Nurofen	Nurofen	Nurofen	Nurofen	Nurofen
Hair care product	Pantene	Pantene	Pantene	Head & Shoulders	Head & Shoulders	Pantene	Pantene
Skin care product	-	Olay	Olay	Olay	Nivea	Nivea	Nivea
Cosmetic	Olay	Boots No7	Boots	Boots	Boots	Boots	Boots
Breakfast cereal	-	-	-	-	-	Kelloggs	Kelloggs
Soap powder	Persil	Persil	Persil	Persil	Persil	Persil	Persil

Table 5. The Reader's Digest trusted UK brand results[lxxxiv]

When I present these research findings, I normally ask the audience whether they agree with the list, and what they feel are the criteria for getting onto, and staying on the list.

3.1.1.2 Inferred/transferred trust

Figure 13 shows the impact of transferred trust in terms of the overall trust someone has towards another person or company.

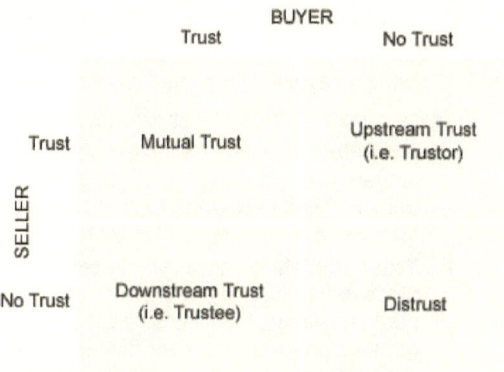

Figure 13. A classification matrix of trust research in relationships between individuals and/or organisations[lxxxv]

The matrix in Figure 13 demonstrates the way in which buyers and sellers interact in terms of trust. When both display and deserve trust, this is *mutual* trust, but if there is trust only with one of the parties, this becomes a one-way trust relationship – called *upstream* or *downstream* by Svensson. Thus when neither side have or display trust, we enter a distrusting relationship. There are a number of levels of trust within each of these areas, all of which are summed up in Figure 14.

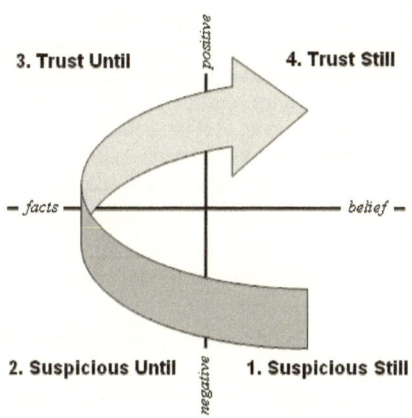

Figure 14. Trust and suspicion[lxxxvi]

1. **Suspicious still**. Do not ever trust anyone, even after they have done something nice
2. **Suspicious until**. Do not trust anyone until they prove themselves
3. **Trust until**. Trust people until they screw up
4. **Trust still**. Trust people even after they make mistakes, sometimes even when they hurt you

Here are some beliefs I have about trust models:

- **Evolution**. Although you might be today in any one of the four stages, you can also move through various stages in life. I like to think that if people start out life in a suspicious stage, that they can evolve to becoming more trusting of others
- **Trust still**. Many people would argue that stage 4 is a bad place to be, trusting people even after they have hurt you or made mistakes. I think it is all a matter of degrees, but in general, prefer to be closer to stage 4 than stage 3. I also do not like working with people who are in stage 1, and often (but not always) do not like working with people who are in stage 2
- **Optimism**. Optimism/belief is a critical component for being very successful. (E.g. sculptor who sees the statue and simply frees it from the stone; Emotional Quotient, the marshmallow test, etc.). I think there is a strong correlation between trust models and optimism
- **Success**. People at the top of the trust diagram are generally more successful in life than those on the bottom. Part of this is that you often need to trust colleagues to have them perform at their highest levels

3.1.2 In-company

Within a company, employees need to trust one another to do their part of the job. For example, in new product development, a marketer will gather the research and customer requirements, and the development engineer/ designer has to trust that all the information is available to develop the product that is required. The marketer must trust that the engineer/designer will use the input to produce the product that the marketer can then launch in the market.

All companies should have customers as their main focus, and this means that all employees must trust one another to have the customers requirements at heart, and that they will do their best for them.

Most companies have some legal frameworks to ensure that employees and partner companies can be trusted, normally in the form of employment contracts and Non-Disclosure Agreements (NDA).

3.1.2.1 Corporate Social Responsibility (CSR)

One way that companies try to demonstrate their trustworthiness is the use of corporate social responsibility programmes. Unfortunately, for some companies this begins and ends with an annual charitable donation. Other companies, however, do look to being a positive influence in their community.

Corporate Social Responsibility (CSR) is a current objective for companies, part of which includes social and legal standards. In most cases, CSR appears to be feel-good activity to the company and its employees, without providing much benefit outside it, more of this later. This is classified as a potential limitation to marketing communications by authors such as Kotler who says, "Creative advertising must not overstep social and legal norms[lxxxvii]." These would be the ethical implications mentioned earlier, but it does not really demonstrate the scope of the issues.

Looking at the marketing mix, the 4P's of Product, Price, Promotion and Place (distribution) that marketers use to guide marketing activities, we can build a model that demonstrates the need to factor in the loyalty and trust to act as gatekeeper to targeted customers. Promoting a new product to a group of customers who lack trust and demonstrate disloyal behaviour, the company will find that the promotion and therefore the product launch is expensive, and very short-term. This is all demonstrated within Figure 15 – showing that trust and loyalty (in this case combined) are factors that can only appear, and be addressed after the development of the 4P's strategies. Later in this book we expand this to the 7P's, which also include People, Physical evidence and Processes.

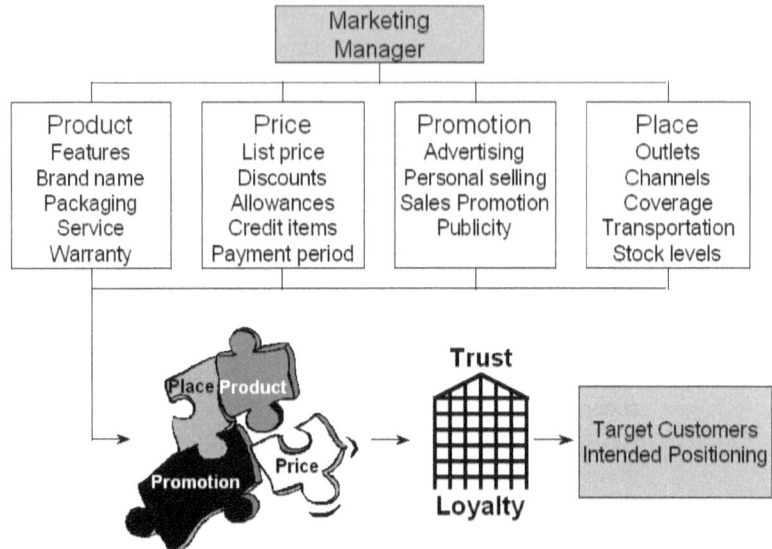

Figure 15. Elements of the marketing mix to the marketplace[lxxxviii]

Ethical behaviour should lead all aspects of the corporate interaction with its customers, past, present and future, providing companies with a competitive advantage. Ideally, ethical behaviour should not only be seen as a potential competitive advantage, but in the harsh business world, the reality is that many companies try to cut corners. In the book 'No Logo,' Naomi Klein opened the eyes of many business people who have traditionally been driven by financial drivers[lxxxix]. One of the main corporate subjects in the book is Nike, who were been accused of exploiting cheap, third world workers in almost slave conditions with no union or health representation, having moved jobs from more regulated, expensive countries.

Mike Brennan suggested that the objectives of business and even the language of business also put business people 'at risk' of unethical conduct, and that the commonly cited moral imperatives and 'rules of thumb' do not adequately equip people to deal with the types of moral dilemmas commonly encountered. Instead, he suggested that, if we want people in business to be ethical rather the merely appear ethical, a completely different paradigm and method of enquiry may be required[xc]. He goes on to say that some people adopt an approach that accepts a need for ethical conduct, but never actually consider the question of ethics because proponents believe they behave ethically; that "good business is good ethics". This view is wrongly reported to have been from Peters & Waterman – they actually reckoned that good ethics is good business[xci]. This is the view taken by this author.

Marketing, as Paul Smith states, was easier when the economy was expanding and consumer disposable income was growing[xcii]. For three decades after World War II, marketing strategies generally were built around the development of growth markets. Satisfying customers was important, but never as important as it has become in the nineties and in to the twenty-first century, with the competitive pressures of largely static markets.

Previously, ethical problems were less apparent, not so much because people did not care, but because society's expectations were different and there was a simple rule for evaluating marketing practices: caveat emptor, was within the rule of law. If it was legal to sell a product that might be harmful or might not live up to the seller's promises, then marketing the product was acceptable because the decision to buy was the consumer's. The consumer was expected to employ the maxim, 'buyer beware.'

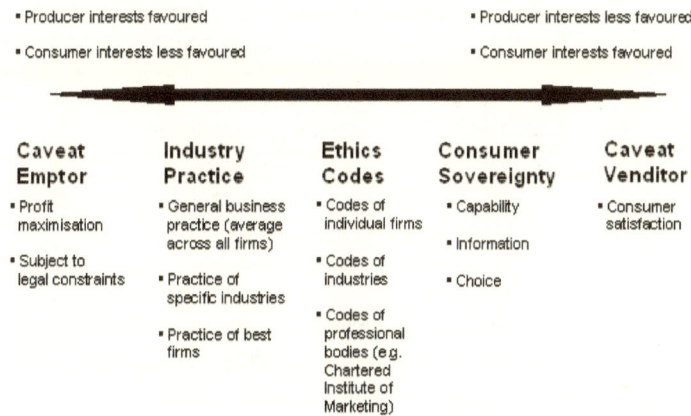

- Producer interests favoured
- Consumer interests less favoured

- Producer interests less favoured
- Consumer interests favoured

Caveat Emptor	Industry Practice	Ethics Codes	Consumer Sovereignty	Caveat Venditor
• Profit maximisation	• General business practice (average across all firms)	• Codes of individual firms	• Capability	• Consumer satisfaction
• Subject to legal constraints	• Practice of specific industries	• Codes of industries	• Information	
	• Practice of best firms	• Codes of professional bodies (e.g. Chartered Institute of Marketing)	• Choice	

Figure 16. Marketing ethics continuum[xciii]

Figure 16 shows the scale of ethics as presented by Smith, demonstrating the drift from *Caveat Emptor* – buyers beware – to *Caveat Venditor* – sellers beware. The latter is certainly becoming the norm on the Internet, and in some cases both apply, for example within eBay, the Internet auction site.

CSR goes further by making the company proactive in its social responsibilities. Many companies believe this is just a case of electing a 'favoured' charity, holding events and making donations. Companies like Ericsson, the mobile phone manufacturer, state the following objectives: "We believe companies should act in a responsible way, maintaining high standards in corporate governance, employee and supplier conduct, sustainability and the environment, and humanitarian aid. Ericsson has signed and accepted the UN Global Compact's nine principles for human rights. We see these principles as a prerequisite for sound, long-term business."

CSR is a case of upholding moral and ethical standards, making the actions of the company transparent to all stakeholders. The Business Impact Review Group or Business in the Community, comprising a number of blue chip companies in Britain[xciv], state their principles as follows:

Responsible business practice must rest in principles integrated into the business and managed throughout its operations. Business in the Community has set out its principles for responsible business practice as:

- To treat employees fairly and equitably
- To operate ethically and with integrity
- To respect basic human rights
- To sustain the environment for future generations

Furthermore, members commit to:

- Integrate responsible business practice throughout the business
- Impact through collaborative action to tackle disadvantage
- Inspire, innovate and lead by sharing learning and experience

This is a group of companies who, together, are leading the way in ethical practices. Some companies are doing this on their own initiative. One such company is the telecommunications company AT&T, who's CSR Policy is worth mentioning here. They aim to:

- Engage in ethical business and governance practices
- Report financial results in a straight forward and candid manner
- Display good corporate citizenship
- Develop and maintain strong customer relationships
- Encourage and respect diversity
- Employ fair workforce/workplace policies and practices
- Protect the environment
- Enforce ethical advertising and sponsorship standards
- Produce and market quality products and services

Overall, another solo effort by Motorola sums up the CSR objectives very well. Their Social & Environmental Statement 2002 states: *"it's about reaching out. It's giving. It's sharing. It's teaching. And it's global. Around the world, our people are making a difference in their communities. We're doing it one hour at a time... volunteering, mentoring, inspiring. We're doing it one dollar at a time... through grants, matching gifts, scholarships, equipment donations and financial support for deserving charities. But all those single hours – all those individual dollars – add up to something big. We take our responsibility to giving back seriously. Motorola is proud to be able to do what we do, and we're proud of our people's passion."*

Some references to ethical practices try to justify unethical practices by claiming that only companies with similar costs, sizes, legal restrictions, etc, can be compared with one another. It is true that companies with deeper pockets can undertake projects such as the CSR programmes discussed in this chapter. Which small company can afford to lose employee time on social projects, or make large donations when they struggle to make ends meet themselves?

The less formal 'rules of thumb' for ethical issues can help employees get in touch with their own feelings and conscience about the decisions that have been made. Peter and Olson provide the following summary:[xcv]

i.   The Golden Rule:
Act in the way that you would expect others to act toward you

ii.   The Professional Ethic:
Take actions that would be viewed as proper by a disinterested panel of professional colleagues

iii.   The TV Test (or Morning Papers Test):
A manager should always ask: "Would I feel comfortable explaining to a national TV audience why I took this action?"

Many companies live by the adage that charity begins at home – understandable as it stands – but there are many other ways in which companies can be socially responsible and ethical without impacting their day-to-day business. Complying with basic ethical standards is something that any company can do and should not cost anything in terms of resources or money.

Ethical development is shown in Figure 17, showing different levels of 'morality', a term often substituted for ethics.

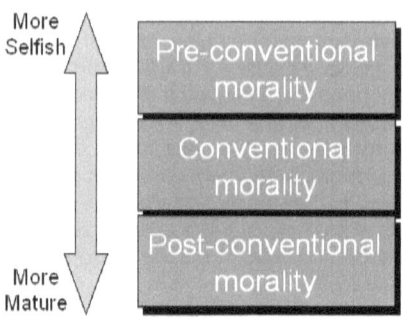

Morality & Business ethics are:

- Childlike
- Based on punishment & reward
- Self-centred, calculating, selfish

- Moves towards the expectations of society
- Concerned over legality & opinions of others
- 'When in Rome, do as the Romans'

- Morality of the mature adult
- Concern about how they judge themselves
- Concern if it is right in the long run

Figure 17. Ethical development levels[xcvi]

In business terms, ethical guidelines within the organisation help to identify acceptable business practices, which may change territory by territory. It also helps control the behaviour of employees and reduces the confusion in decision making by facilitating a discussion about what is right and wrong in the eyes of the customer. Based on this, a model can be made of the CSR hierarchy, see Figure 18.

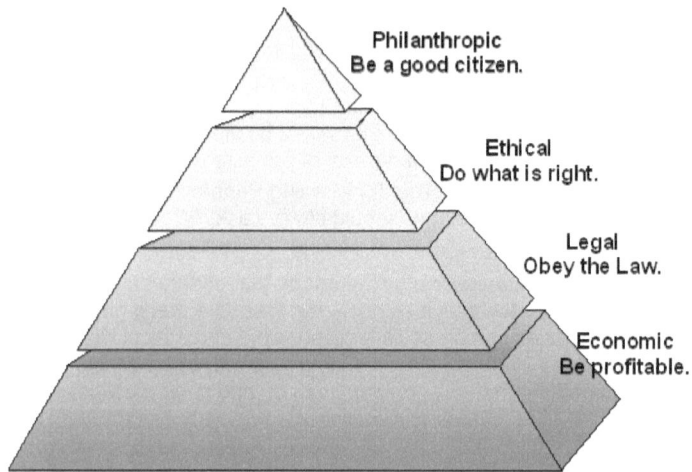

Figure 18. Hierarchy of corporate social responsibility[xcvii]

As with all hierarchical representations, the lower elements, in the case of Figure 18 – economics and legality – are hygiene factors, ethics are something to strive for before a company can be regarded as philanthropic.

International standards are another matter, and will be discussed in more detail later. When operating internationally, the strictest guidelines - whether legal or ethical - should be adhered to, which may increase costs, but offer greater overall rewards.

Smith also quotes Laczniak and his ethical maxims, as follows:
In evaluating the ethics of their marketing practices, marketers often rely on simple maxims. Though useful, they generally lack specific guidance. Some common maxims are:

- Do unto others what you would have them do unto you
  This is not necessarily correct, as the most important factor is the way the customers expect to be treated – this may not be the same way as you would want to be treated, though it is normally a good guide

- Would I be embarrassed in front of colleagues/family/friends if the media publicised my decision? (The TV test mentioned earlier)

- Are there any payments that could not be fully disclosed in company accounts?

- Good ethics is in the firm's long-term best interests

- Would an objective panel of professional colleagues view this action as proper?

When in doubt, don't[xcviii]McClenahen points out that experts identify the following as operating principles specifically for e-ethics:

- Be aware of cultural differences
  Sometimes ethical issues on one continent are normal business practices in another

- Don't settle for the lowest common denominator
  Hold yourself and your company to the highest combination of ethical standards in the countries where you do business

- Provide a choice
  Let Internet customers decide whether or not you can capture data on them. Providing the option often results in customers offering more information than they would otherwise

- Be trustworthy
  Be 100% truthful and deliver everything you are offering

- Make ethics count
  With leadership coming from top management, upgrade ethical standards 'across the board' and make them part of a rewards structure[xcix]

If the Internet is going to be the prime marketplace of the future, an article of American newspaper, 'The Star', stated it should then be governed by business laws and should incorporate "honourable" business practices. In short, the Internet economy should adopt business ethics.

3.1.3 Building trust

So how does one build trust? Commercially, and personally, this involves demonstrating trustworthiness. This, of course is easier in some professions and industries than in others.

When a company starts in business, the nature of the business will start to define the trustworthiness of the business. In the UK, used car sales have an image of attracting untrustworthy, almost criminal elements. Therefore a trustworthy trader setting up in this industry would have to shake off the industry image – in relation to Figure 9, the trust lifecycle – the trust actually starts below the zero on the vertical axis.

In this case, however, a trustworthy trader could benefit from even greater transferred trust, if the market is desperate for used cars form a trustworthy source.

Assuming your company/business is in a completely new, unclassified marketplace (it is difficult to comprehend such a market, as customers will always try to classify a product, service or business into the world they are comfortable with). In such a situation, customers will base their perceptions on the brand and personal characteristics being presented to them. In chapter 4 we will introduce the concept of friendship as a means of ethical and trustworthy sales. If customers see you as a friend, you are more likely to build trust.

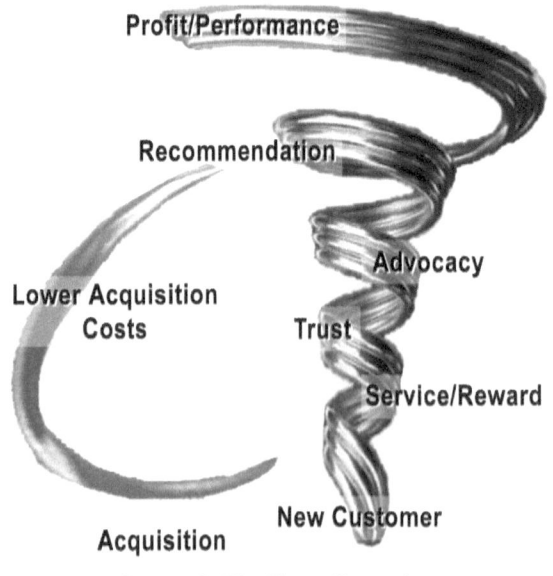

Figure 19. The Trust Tornado

The Trust Tornado (Figure 19) shows the influence of trust within a customer acquisition/retention system, such as a CRM programme. New customers are (hopefully) sucked up into the vortex. If the vortex is too weak, the customers will fall straight back down without an experience of the brand, or worse still, a bad experience.

If the customer remains, they are forced upwards into the vortex to experience the additional services and rewards offered. This in turn should generate an element of trust and advocacy. At any time within this vortex, a customer could fall if the pressure is not maintained.

When an advocate recommends new customers, as we have seen in Figure 9, the new customers will gain trust and become advocates far faster, all at a lower acquisition cost. In the tornado analogy, the downdrafts help feed the upward movement of the vortex.

The stronger the vortex is, the greater the profit and performance rewards the brand can expect. But, as with any tornado, a lack of 'fuel' cause them to die. It is up to the company marketers to keep feeding the tornado, possibly creating multiple spouts to transfer customers to new, stronger products.

3.1.3.1 Loyalty

Loyalty has been a trend of the last ten years, with many retail companies setting up loyalty schemes. Unfortunately, they do not breed loyalty amongst customers, as the customers are more likely to be members of many competing loyalty programmes.

So how does a company build loyalty? In Figure 15, loyalty and trust were combined as a gate, or filter. It could be argued that true loyalty cannot exist without trust. If a customer is loyal to the brand or product, they are more likely to trust the company, and probably be a strong advocate of that company.

Conversely, a lack of trust will lead to a lack of loyalty towards the brand. This, of course, is clouded by modern loyalty programmes where customers are looking for benefits, such as free give-aways and discounts, from the necessity of having to shop with a particular retailer.

3.1.3.1.1 Satisfaction

Customer satisfaction is also a result of trust; as a trusting relationship will provide the customer with greater satisfaction, and provide the company with a greater understanding should problems arise.

The link between satisfaction and trust provides a virtuous circle for the relationship, as a company will remain profitable during this cycle and the customer will continue to return to that product, brand or company as a trusted partner.

3.1.3.1.2 Without trust

Companies who do not engender trust amongst their customers face a more difficult task for new product or service, and generally to persuade customers to part with their money. A senior Downing Street adviser stated that the willingness of British people to trust each other halved over the past 40 years[c].

The Guardian newspaper reported a research finding on trust in European institutions. The European Union has published the results of its latest Eurobarometer survey of public opinion in the 25 European member states. Perhaps it is no surprise to discover that Britain once again comes at the bottom of the trust table in attitudes towards the EU. Just 26% of us trust the EU, compared with a not overly impressive 45% of the European population as a whole. What is most striking of all, though, is that the gap between the UK and the next most mistrustful nation (Sweden) is so large, 12 points. This suggests that we live in a world of our own.

Because it's not just the EU we don't trust. We don't trust our own government either. The Eurobarometer survey found that just 24% of Britons trust the British government - a six point fall in just six months, by the way. It's true that we finished above the Hungarians (whose government admitted this year that it had lied to them about the economic situation) and the Poles (whose government has become a byword for incompetence at home and abroad) and on the same score as Jacques Chirac's broken-backed French government. But there's a pattern here that can't be overlooked. We are 25th out of 25 on trust for the EU, 22nd out of 25 on trust for our national government, and 19th out of 25 in trust for our national parliament. Trustwise, we are the Watford of the western world.

And don't try to kid yourself that this is all just about politicians. Our net of mistrust is cast far wider than that. When Eurobarometer measured the level of trust in the press, Britain was back once again in our accustomed 25th and last place. A mere 19% of people in this country trust the press, compared with a European average of 44%. The next lowest score in this league is by Hungary, where 32% do not trust the press. Note the gap between their score and ours. Once again, it suggests there is something exceptional about Britain.

Of course even the British trust some people more than others. Earlier this year the Committee on Standards in Public Life commissioned some Mori research on attitudes towards public institutions and conduct. It found that 93% of us trust doctors, that 84% trust head teachers and that 81% of us trust judges. It found that we differentiate between television news journalists, whom a narrow majority of Britons trust, and tabloid newspaper journalists, who are trusted by only 9%. We trust our local MP more than MPs in general and we trust both more than we trust government ministers. We even trust estate agents more than we trust ministers[ci].

The most graphic business example of the failure of trust comes form the Enron collapse. Enron was a trusted and respected company who went on to abuse the trust the market placed in them. Their auditors, the accountancy firm Arthur Andersen were also caught up in the scandal, and despite having numerous other customers, this one indiscretion caused customers to leave them in droves, leading to their own bankruptcy.

It is always possible that a company can exist without any trust exhibited from customers, suppliers or backers, but not from all of these stakeholders. Every company does aim to build the trust of their stakeholders, but some do not see trust as a strategic goal.

3.1.3.2 Culture

Culture plays a huge part in the ethics and therefore the trust that is displayed by customers and other stakeholders. We have examined the cultural impact in ethics, but trust is just as important. The Greek philosopher Plato defined a group of countries within a loose republic whereby each were weak in certain areas, but masters of a particular task. The republic would then be built on mutual co-operation and trust amongst the States[cii].

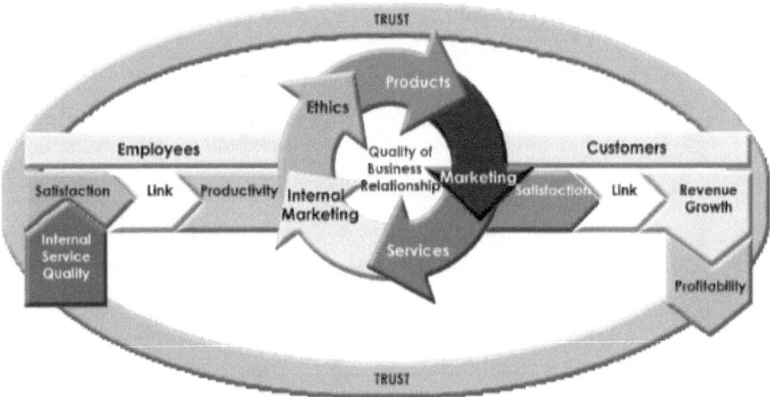

Figure 20. The virtuous circle of trust within an organisation

The virtuous circle of trust shown in Figure 20 shows that the quality of business relationships come from a combination of employees and customers. Everything the relationship does (or does not do) is supported by a culture of trust. The employees will feel more satisfied and fulfilled from their work, and the customers will be satisfied by the relationship they have with the company.

Companies that exhibit a trustworthy manner are more likely to win their customer's long term trust and respect. One of the ways in which this can be facilitated is by adopting a open and honest communications process – not that the customer will know if they are told everything, honestly, but it must appear like that in the eyes of the customers.

3.1.3.3 Value chain

To this end, I have taken Michael Porter's famous value chain model and adapted it to demonstrate the trust-focused value chain, as shown in Figure 21.

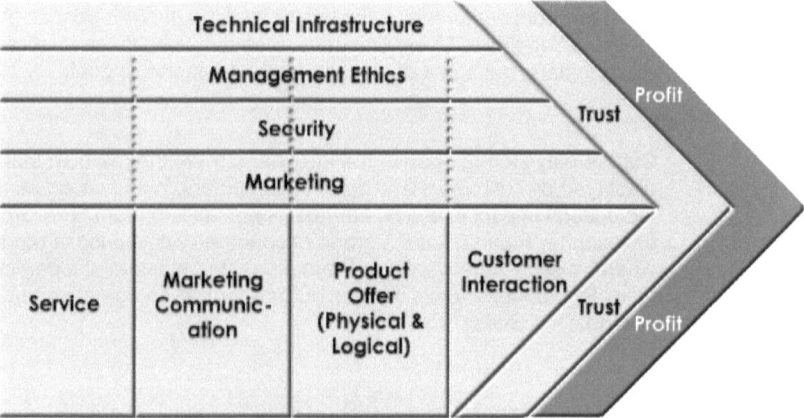

Figure 21. The trust-focused value chain model[ciii]

The model shows a number of marketing activities that a company does that can influence the level of trust held by customers. Some of these activities are intangible, so branding and 'public' relations are extremely important.

It is also interesting to note that the element of 'trust' replaces that of profit in Porter's original model, although I have also included a second arrow called profit as it can be proven that consumer trust does drive profit, in other words, being trustworthy is profitable!

3.1.3.3.1 Competitive advantage

Every company tries to get a competitive advantage to provide a foundation for their branding and brand character. Porter originally identified the competitive advantage of nations and companies, and looked at companies gaining an advantage from cost leadership, differentiation or focus. It can be argued that a trust focus can be a competitive advantage if done correctly, and a failure to address matters of trust can give others an advantage.

3.1.3.4 Need for trust

It is obvious that a company must have the trust of its customers, and it is part of the human character to trust and to expect to trust. As such, trust is part of a need, hence the reference to Abraham Maslow who studied the hierarchy of needs.

Figure 22 shows the amended value drivers tree as they apply to Maslow's hierarchy of needs, demonstrating that trust is one of the higher hygiene factors, as opposed a differentiation factor.

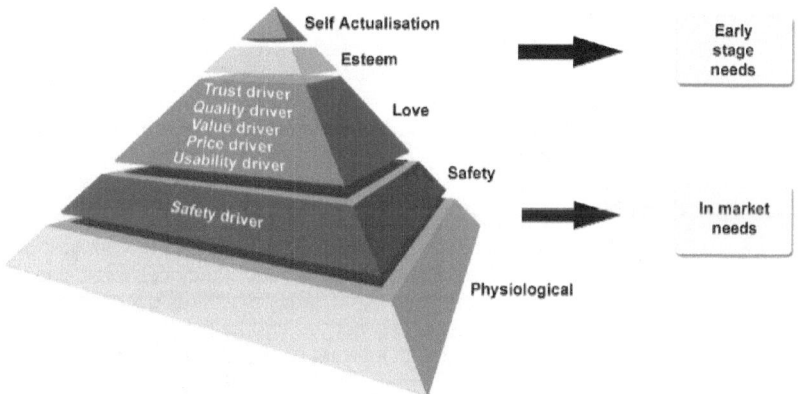

Figure 22. Customer value drivers model[civ]

In Figure 22, we see that in contrast to Maslow's theory on the development of needs within the hierarchy, the value drivers almost work in an opposite direction, with the customer wanting or expecting the needs of self-actualisation and esteem at the early stages of the relationship. This means that the trust driver is one of the early requirements, and that a customer must have some form of trust in the company. This is the opposite of Figure 9 in which the trust grows over time, starting from an untrusting relationship.

One of the possible explanations of this may be that this model represents the modern luxury product market. In such a market, the fashion and look of the product generally overrides the practicalities, such as the safety. One would certainly need some level of trust, but as in diagram 9, this will grow over time. This means that unlike Maslow's theory that shows a chronological movement up to self-actualisation, the customer value driver's model demonstrates the customer's aspirations, and if a product or service appeals to them, the product will appeal in the early stages. Continued consumption of the product/service will show its worth, and therefore start including other, more basic needs.

3.1.4 Destroying trust

There is a saying, "it takes years to build trust, and a few seconds to destroy it[cv]." The Enron example is not unique, but is still fresh in most minds. It is however, not the act of breaking the trust of the customers, many other companies and individuals have done that in the past, it is how they react to it. A remorseful company that tries everything to rectify the problems will probably build increased trust in its brand and its policies, whereas a company who demonstrate that it was a risk too far, and that they have no remorse for what had happened will lose the trust and respect of their customers and the marketplace in general.

3.1.4.1 Association

The Enron/Arthur Andersen association is the example everyone sites for destruction of trust by association. Andersen's were the trusted auditors, and initially suffered by association when Enron collapsed. Unfortunately, whilst this association may have been manageable, they were also then found to have been party to the fraud. Andersen fell as customers rapidly disassociated themselves with the fraudulent auditors.

Another form of association was then addressed, following Andersen's decline. Many of the Management/Accountancy consultancies then sold off their management consultancy divisions, distancing themselves from business practices that help run the companies, due to the potential conflicts of interest highlighted by the Enron collapse.

3.1.4.2 Media Abuse

Abuse of the media is another trustbuster. An organisation that consistently manipulates the media to deliver its messages builds scepticism and disbelief amongst its publics.

A graphic example of this is the government 'spin machine' in the UK. There appears to be great distrust in the British political system following consistent manipulation by the Labour government of Tony Blair, and his so-called 'spin-doctor', Alistair Campbell. One of the problems with the manipulation of the media is that the public disbelieve much of the communication from the government. The accusation about 'sexing up' the Iraqi invasion document and the subsequent witch hunt of the BBC for inaccurate reporting of this, and the death of a respected government scientist, have all increased the distrust the UK population have in their governing politicians.

This all fuels the distrust debate outlined by the Guardian article in section 3.1.3.1.2.

3.1.4.2.1 Spam

Using electronic media, such as websites and e-mail has been one of the fastest growing phenomena in the modern world. Unfortunately, there are people who, given such an opportunity, look at it as a means of exploiting loopholes and practice illegal activities.

When we talk of abuse of electronic communications we generally mean 'spam'. This generic term has been adopted to denote any unsolicited communication. It is thought to originate from the Monty Python comedy sketch in which every dish offered at a café involved differing quantities of spam.

There is an attempt to outlaw the use of this term by the owners of the trademark – Hormel Foods Corp., the makers of the luncheon meat product. They have tried to clamp down on the secondary meaning of the word by taking proceedings against Spam Arrest LLC, a Seattle-based technology company that sells e-mail filtering software. The claim is that the trademark is being diluted by use of this secondary meaning, and the associated confusion between the food product and the electronic product is damaging the goodwill and reputation of the original spam. Unfortunately, the term 'spam' is already deeply engrained in the Internet culture now, despite attempts to combat it, and it is interesting that they did not object to Monty Python!

Junk mail originated long before the Internet (as with most of these abuses), but the high costs of production and distribution was a limiting factor. The Internet has provided a much faster and lower cost medium, so unsolicited mailings have grown exponentially. Organisations such as the Direct Marketing Association in the USA, and the Institute of Direct Marketing in the UK, helped regulate the industry, and because of the costs involved, many adhered to the guidelines.

The Internet, with its apparent anonymity, low cost distribution and speed to market, has given the authorities a legal and ethical headache. Because the Internet spans the globe, it is unclear which laws apply and who is responsible for it's policing. Some countries have put a totalitarian block on the Internet, whilst others believe in allowing completely free expression online.

Alex Salkever says, "the real solution [against spam] lies in stripping e-mail of anonymity[cvi]." Certainly, anonymity allows spammers to hide their identity behind any number of aliases, avoiding national efforts to combat excessive and unwanted e-mails.

The first recorded spam e-mail message was sent in 1992. This was a relatively innocent act at the time, but it proved the reach of the medium, even in those days.

It may be the first recorded commercial spam but it was certainly not the origin of the term. Spam and spamming were common terms in MUDs (Multiple User Dimension, Multiple User Dungeon, or Multiple User Dialogue is a computer program which users can log into and explore) several years before Cantor and Siegel, Immigration Attorneys, and the word spam was often included in the subject of usenet (A worldwide bulletin board system that can be accessed through the Internet or through many online services. The USENET contains more than 14,000 forums, called newsgroups, which cover every imaginable interest group) test messages. A fairly common early meaning was the practice of creating lots of traffic, which interrupted a machine or network. In 1992 there are references to e-mail spamming and spamming newsgroups, which is what Cantor and Siegel later did.[cvii]

First Commercial Spam

From: Laurence Canter (nike@indirect.com)
Subject: Green Card Lottery- Final One?
Newsgroups: alt.brother-jed, alt.pub.coffeehouse.amethyst
View: Complete Thread (4 articles) | Original Format
Date: 1994-04-12 00:40:42 PST

Green Card Lottery 1994 May Be The Last One!
THE DEADLINE HAS BEEN ANNOUNCED.

The Green Card Lottery is a completely legal program giving away a certain annual allotment of Green Cards to persons born in certain countries. The lottery program was scheduled to continue on a permanent basis. However, recently, Senator Alan J Simpson introduced a bill into the U. S. Congress which could end any future lotteries. THE 1994 LOTTERY IS SCHEDULED TO TAKE PLACE SOON, BUT IT MAY BE THE VERY LAST ONE.

PERSONS BORN IN MOST COUNTRIES QUALIFY, MANY FOR FIRST TIME.

The only countries NOT qualifying are: Mexico; India; P.R. China; Taiwan, Philippines, North Korea, Canada, United Kingdom (except Northern Ireland), Jamaica, Dominican Republic, El Salvador and Vietnam.

Lottery registration will take place soon. 55,000 Green Cards will be given to those who register correctly. NO JOB IS REQUIRED.

THERE IS A STRICT JUNE DEADLINE. THE TIME TO START IS NOW!!

For FREE information via E-mail, send request to cslaw@indirect.com

--
****
Canter & Siegel, Immigration Attorneys
3333 E Camelback Road, Ste 250, Phoenix AZ 85018 USA
cslaw@indirect.com telephone (602) 661-3911 Fax (602) 451-7617

The first acknowledged commercial spam e-mail[cviii]

Much has been said about 'Canning the Spam' – the US 'legislation'. In Europe, legislation is attempting to stop it, with the threat of large fines and long prison sentences; even the USA is starting to adopt legislative measures to block spammers. But, as pointed out by Salkever, everything we do to stop it may, perversely make spam even harder to stop, in the same way that over used antibiotics have helped create stronger viruses and bugs[cix]. A recent article by the BBC highlighted the new trend of hijacking personal computers with Trojan viruses (apparently safe applications and/or cookies that reside on the machine until they are activated and allow third party access to that machine). Spammers are using hacker's tricks to cover their tracks and reduce the chances of blocking messages[cx].

But what exactly is spam and why do people do it? Spam is unsolicited, in other words not requested by the individual. It is usually a flood of many copies of the same message that has one of two objectives;
1) to force the users to express an interest in, or buy the products or services on offer (although in many cases no products are available, though money is taken!), and
2) to validate the person's e-mail address to sell onto other spammers for increased sums of money. This is borne out by the content of many spam messages that offer dubious products, prescription drugs, get-rich-quick schemes, quasi-legal services or pornography.

One of the reasons spam is so attractive to the sender, is that the sending costs are very low, and in most cases the costs of downloading, storing and fighting spam is borne by the receiver. Some messages have a 'Please remove me from your list' link at the bottom of the e-mail – unfortunately, this normally just validates the e-mail address to create a tidal wave of spam.

3.1.4.2.2 The 419 scam

One line of spamming that has caught the attention of the public media is the '419' scam. This is named after the legislative code that it contravenes in Nigeria, the original source of many of these messages.

This is a scam that started in the 1920's, long before the birth of the Internet, and involves a letter (now also e-mail) being sent, privately and confidentially, to the recipient asking for their help in getting money out of Nigeria (or any other country – I have seen Lagos, South Africa and Zimbabwe recently), all for a generous commission. All you need to do for them is provide your banking details and in some cases some money up front as a bribe for the 'local' officials.

Amazingly, about 75 people are defrauded every year in Britain alone, to the value of about £8 million! One ring participating in this fraud was recently arrested in Amsterdam, with all the latest technology. Steve Fox of PCWorld magazine stated that this scam was an e-mail administered IQ test. If you fail you can join DENSA (Dupes Exploited by Nigerian Scam Artists)[cxi]!

3.1.4.2.3 The prospects for spam

Spam is being targeted as an anti-social activity, indeed, if not checked, it could kill e-mail as a communications medium. Bill Gates, CEO of Microsoft recently announced that they were looking at introducing a type of 'postage' fee for all e-mail traffic. This may well work, except that the spammers need not have a high response rate to recoup their costs. It would certainly reduce his four million messages per day, making him the most 'spammed' person in the world[cxii]. It could, however reduce the number of spammers active in the world, but as the majority of spam is thought to be generated by just a handful of people, it is questionable if this will work. The 'snail-mail' postage system requires a postage fee, but how often is a letter delivered with insufficient or no fee on it? Would this also happen online? And what if your machine has one of the Trojan spamming engines on it – you will be charged as a spammer, and the real criminal will still reap whatever rewards are on offer.

One suggestion is that the adoption of 'white lists' could end spam. A white list is a list of approved senders that would be stored on a PC or on the e-mail server and block any messages that came from anyone other that on the list. This would certain curtail the efforts of many spammers, but if they infiltrate a home PC, they could assume the identity of that person and send spam to addresses stored on that computer, and therefore on the white listing!

If we do manage to kill the spam-trade on e-mail, it is highly likely that they will move onto other channels. We have already seen a rise in SMS spam. Messages telling users that they have won prizes, or need to contact customer service, or dial a certain number for a voice-mail, are all spam, and generally involve the user phoning a premium rate number.

My experience of this is that these messages arrive on a Friday evening, and that the company running the so-called promotion is no longer 'trading' by the Monday morning, thus avoiding any chance of being stopped during their scam. The mobile phone companies are playing catch-up with this sort of scam and there is good chance that this will increase if unchecked. The advancement of technology to allow pictures, audio and visual clips and hyperlinks to be sent using MMS will most likely offer even more opportunities for spamming.

3.1.4.2.4 Flaming

Flaming is a newsgroup term for a vicious response to inaccuracies, slander or other such behaviour. It normally involves the originator of the comment being bombarded with abusive e-mails or responses in an attempt to deter them from returning to the newsgroup. This has, however been extended to spammers; another name for it is mail-bombing.

In most cases, newsgroup moderators would remove the original comments to try to avoid any escalation. But we are seeing an increasing number of character and/or brand assassinations, otherwise known as cybersmearing.

The publication of untrue statements that damage the reputation of a person, business or its products or services could be considered defamation or disparagement. Zugelder *et al,* states that web marketers are considered 'publishers', such online libel would be judged in the same way as any other mass media advertising medium[cxiii]. They point out the use of the Internet as a breeding ground for consumer dissatisfaction. For example, a Yahoo! search on the words 'hate' and 'sucks' came up with over 600 hits related to 'corporate' sites[cxiv] – including sites such as ToysRUs Sucks, I Hate McDonalds, etc. Six years on from this study, Yahoo! now returns over 42 million sites.

Disgruntled employees are also using the Internet to spread rumours about their companies, creating a direct negative affect on stock prices, and in some cases slandering the executives. Many of these people get away with such activities because of the anonymity of the web. Cybersmearing can take a number of different forms including websites, message boards, e-mail and auctions.

However, a recent case in Canada involving Vaquero Energy & Waldner v. Nick Weir found information that was traced back to Weir, and ended in Weir being liable for defamation[cxv].

Vaquero Energy & Waldner v. Nick Weir 2004.

The case concerned a financial message board known as Stockgroup and Vaquero, an oil and gas company in Calgary, Canada. Waldner was Vaquero's CEO, hired to consolidate the business. In 2002 Waldner became aware of a number of messages on Stockgroup's site from two anonymous posters, which accused Waldner of being 'insane, retarded, managing the company for his own benefit' and compared him to Osama bin Laden, Hitler and Saddam Hussein. 48 messages were discovered sent over a four-month period.

The messages were eventually tracked back to Weir, who had spoken to Waldner a couple of times and written to ask for a place on Vaquero's board. Proceedings were served on Weir and the postings stopped the day they were served. Weir then stated a class action lawsuit against the company. Weir said the messages were not his, but the court heard detailed evidence against him, including evidence related to the IP addresses and the use by both of the anonymous posters of 123456 as their password.

The judge found Weir liable for defamation. She said that there was no evidence of financial damage to Vaquero and ordered Weir to pay it CA$10,000. But the messages directed at Waldner had caused him real concern and he was awarded CA$40,000 in damages. Punitive damages were also awarded of CA$25,000.

Some 'flaming' or cybersmearing could be because of retaliation, returning the abuse suffered on newsgroup noticeboards or in chat rooms. This is, of course, counter-productive as some aggressors could be seen as the victim and will be free to continue the practice on others. In the same way as the anti-spam advice is to do nothing retaliatory, the same advice can be given for this practice.

3.1.4.2.5 Cookies

No, not the biscuits, but the 'crumbs' that are placed on a computer when a user enters a website. Cookies are an important tool in the usability of websites, best summed up by the Motley Fool website [sic]:

> If you went to the same pub, day after day, year after year, and every time the barman had to ask you your name and what your drink was, you'd be a bit annoyed. Well, we want this website to be like a friendly neighbourhood local, where the barman calls you by your name and has a cold mug of your favourite beer (or whatever) in front of you before your backside hits the barstool.
>
> Sounds very personable, so 'take me back to the home page'.[cxvi]

The benefits are clear to those of us who develop and build websites. Marketers also see the benefit of identifying a 'known face' as they enter the site, as they can target relevant products, services and content to that user.

Customers, however, appear to be concerned by the 'spy' image the cookies conjure up, allowing the cookie owner to track every move on the site, knowing where the user has come from and goes to. In most cases this is done in any case, anonymously for statistical purposes – you will hear website owners talking about statistics of Page Impressions (PI), Unique Visitors (UV), session length, pages per session, PI per UV and frequency of return.

There may well be some websites that do spy on the user, but it is only possible within the domain, or in associated domains. There was a case where an American website employed Amazon, the online bookstore, to undertake their e-commerce functions. Customers entering this site were confronted with a page that appeared to know their buying habits in an unassociated domain. The e-commerce pages were, of course, looking for the cookies associated with it, and therefore displayed the Amazon information. This was subsequently rectified to avoid customer confusion.

There are two basic versions of cookies; session cookies that are active during the browsing session; and permanent cookies that, as the name implies, are activated as soon as the customer enters the website. The latter version of cookie is the one that causes most concern as they could be activated at any time, as in the Amazon example.

The new data protection rulings in Europe also cover the use of cookies, and the information contained therein. This does, however, only apply to websites that adhere to European rules, sites hosted in other parts of the world are not subject to the same regulations, and therefore could abuse the system.

Abuse is possible using e-media, as with any other media, but technology is removing many opportunities for fraudsters and criminals. It is, ultimately, the responsibility of Internet and e-mail users to ensure that they do not put themselves in danger. I recently devised a board game to teach young children mobile phone safety, and in this we reinforce the points by teaching children not to hand out their e-mail addresses or mobile phone numbers to unknown people. Unfortunately, as we get older we forget that it can be dangerous to talk to strangers!

Abuse is on the increase, but so is the use of the media. With more users on the web, and more opportunities to access the web and e-mails, the abuse is bound to increase. Though spam seems to be increasing exponentially, as the technology improves the delivery mechanisms, that same technology is working hard to track and block the spammers activities.

The fraudsters use every opportunity possible, thus the 419 scam, general spam, misused cookies and spyware that they use. The industry will eradicate most of the abuses, but the question will be whether the abuse will kill the medium first.

3.1.4.2.6 Spyware

As the name suggests, spyware is put on to a computer to spy on what is happening. One example of this could be that it records every keystroke, transmitting this back to the hacker who installed the spyware in the first place.

You may have noticed than may bank and e-commerce sites have a number of pull-down lists for information such as date of birth. This is to combat the possible use of spyware keystroke programmes, as they do not know where on a pull down list the user has clicked.

Spyware can also rack exactly what sites a surfer visits and can report this back to a 'marketer' who can then use this information to augment any other information they possess, making it even more valuable when sold to others – normally without the knowledge of the individual.

There are many programmes now available that will stop or suppress the installation, operation and communication of spyware software. And this is becoming increasingly popular on computers.

3.1.4.2.7 Trojans

There are, however, other forms of spyware, called Trojans, after the Greek story of the Trojan wars. Some of these Trojans could even give control of your computer to a third party. This is becoming more of an issue in the UK where more people are now connected to Broadband (ADSL) and leave their computers and therefore the connections on and open at all times.

Trojans, like the Trojan horse after which they are named, are installed by spyware, or when the user installs some other software. Once installed, it can either start altering processes and data, or it lays dormant, waiting for a trigger. This trigger can be within its own programming, or from an external source – again an issue for those people with an always-on connection to the web.

A popular Trojan operation is to use the host computer as a clone to e-mail spam to others. This is normally done by sending a trigger over the web with information on the message and the possible list to spam. The PC is then sending thousands of e-mails without the knowledge of the user, and avoiding the normal controls against spammers that identify multiple mails from a single machine.

B – Tactical Ethics

4.   Planning

4.1 Communications

Communications are obviously the main means of interacting with our customers. Without a communications strategy we are unlikely to be able to tell our customers how trustworthy we feel we are, and give them any reasons to trust us.

Promotion is part of the marketing mix, which will be explored in more detail later in this chapter. The communications mix includes the following elements:

- Personal selling
- Advertising
- Sales promotion
- Direct marketing
- Publicity (and public relations)
- Sponsorship
- Exhibitions
- Packaging
- Point-of-sales (POS) and merchandising
- Internet
- Word of mouth (including 'viral' marketing)
- Corporate identity[cxvii]

Fill identified the acronym DRIP for marketing communications, to demonstrate the uses to which it can be put.

D   Differentiate products and services

R   Remind and reassure customers and potential customers

I   Inform

P   Persuade targets to think or act in a particular way[cxviii]

With this in mind, there are a number of models that have been developed to demonstrate the way in which people and companies communicate.

4.1.1 Communications model

One would expect communication to be a simple task, after all, we all communicate with one another on a daily basis. This is, unfortunately, too simplified a view. As the models in this section show, external factors play a huge role, confusing, misinforming and drowning out the message.

4.1.1.1 Linear communications

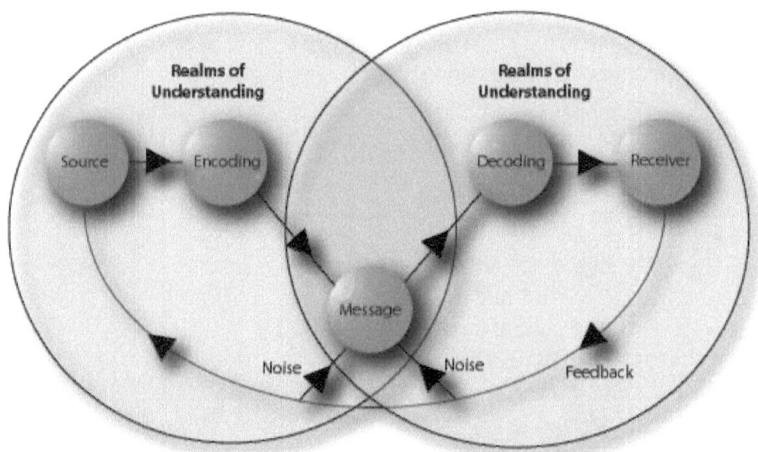

Figure 23. A linear model of communication[cxix]

In the linear model of communication (see Figure 23), the sender encodes a message in verbal, written or symbolic form to pass onto the receiver who can, on receipt, decode the message. Obviously there could be a problem with the understanding of the two parties on the coding principles, such as making a message too cryptic, obscure or confusing.

Assuming the message is delivered in a way that is understood correctly by both parties, thee is a further complication – that of noise which distorts or blocks the message. In the modern world, noise is one of the most important obstacles in the destruction of communications.

Noise can take many different forms, but the main one in the modern electronic world is one of overload. It was reported that the average American is exposed to about 3,000 advertising messages a day, and that, globally, corporations spend over $620 billion each year to make their products seem desirable and to get us to buy them[cxx]."

With such a cacophony of advertising is it any wonder that the customer is going deaf? Especially when we see much of this advertising being poorly targeted or, as in the case of digital marketing and spam, utterly irrelevant and even downright disgusting.

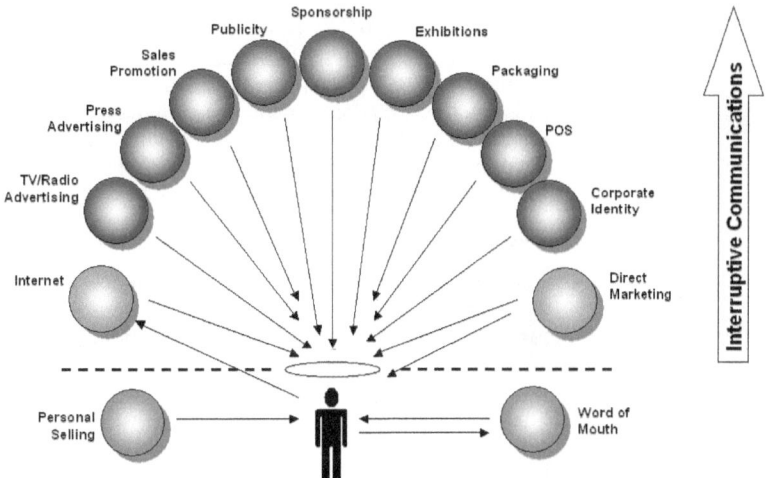

Figure 24. The interruption marketing model[cxxi]

Figure 24 demonstrates the interruption marketing practices confronting the modern consumer (private or business). This is adapted from the concept of interruption marketing by Seth Godin whereby he laments the lack of targeted message thanks to the use of mass marketing techniques, which he claims interrupts the average person continuously.

In this diagram, the darker discs at the top of the diagram show the untargeted, scatter-gun communications channels, moving down to the light discs above the dotted line which can be either – the Internet is mass marketing, but due to the interactivity and the 'pull marketing' character of the medium, this could be seen as a direct channel. Direct marketing too, can be carefully targeted and very relevant to the customer, as Godin points out[cxxii]. But as the spam debate shows, badly targeted direct marketing is just as bad, if not worse than the mass marketing methods. All the indirect, mass marketing channels are filtered through the ring above the customer, forcing many of the messages together, increasing the possible noise and distorting the message.

The darker discs at the top of the diagram, however, provide the customer with direct and relevant communications, although even these can be abused and misused. But the personal touch is normally a means of making a message more relevant and targeted.

This is the big problem facing the Internet and electronic communications in general. Not only are we dealing with local customers, but also potentially, we can attract customers worldwide and hence any communications may miss the mark. Systems such as e-CRM (electronic customer relationship management) try to provide a means of personalisation. This can work well if the company has a good picture of the customer, but if information is missing, assumed or aggregated, this could be just as bad as mass marketing.

4.1.2 Response models

A model was developed in the early days of marketing, to demonstrate the stages that a salesperson must take in the personal selling process[cxxiii]. Since then, numerous commentators have addressed the issue, as can be seen in Table 6.

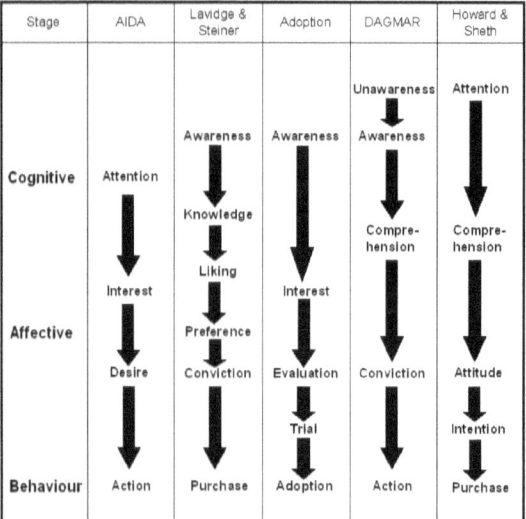

Table 6. The response hierarchy model matrix[cxxiv]

These models assume a customer who has never heard of the product or brand – starting from a point of unawareness towards the company. It is said that these models can be used by marketers to build repeat purchases from profitable customers, only they make no mention of this.

Another model, recently published is more respectful of the prospect or customer.

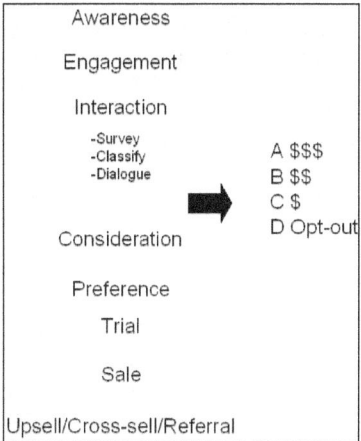

Figure 25. A new model for a new day[cxxv]

The model in Figure 25 was presented by Richard Rosen at the IDM conference in 2005. In this he complained the traditional models – Table 6 – failed to quantify the relationship with the customer. I would agree with this, to a point. A sales person will understand this model and work with it. A marketer, on the other hand does not necessarily always want the customer to part with money – indeed it could be said that not selling to a customer is a positive trust building activity. To this end, I have developed the following model.

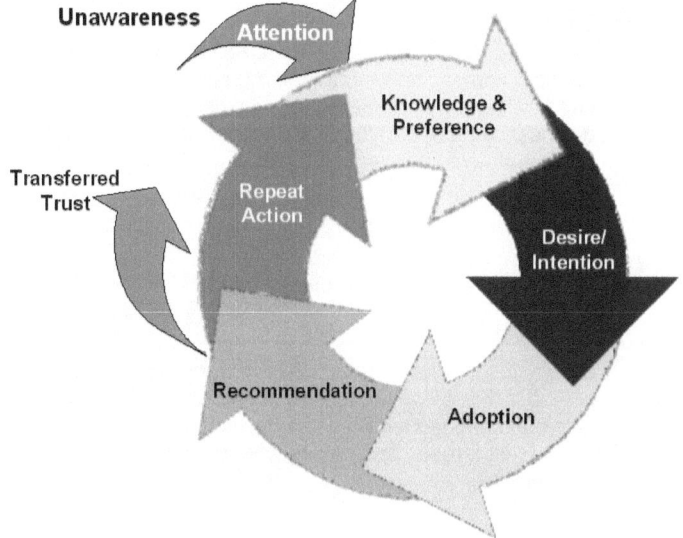

Figure 26. The customer interaction model[cxxvi]

In the customer interaction model, the customer may come from a state of unawareness, to grow some knowledge and preference towards the brand or product. This should then be translated into a state of desire and intent to undertake an action. It is most likely that this action is a purchase, but the important next stage is the adoption. This adoption could be physically purchasing and using the product or service, or it could be adopting the preference and aspiration to own the product. An example of this stage could be the ownership of a Ferrari sports car. Many of us would love to own one, and have reached the desire/intention stage, but the adoption stage lacks the financial capacity, so the adoption is the aspiration, that once affordable, may translate in a purchase.

Following the adoption of the brand or product/service, the customer would be expected to become an advocate of the products, etc., recommending it to other customers, transferring goodwill and trust to the other customers and making them aware of the product. The transferred trust continues to build the brand or market share, whilst the original customer is encouraged, either through their own conviction or by targeted marketing communications, to repeat the action of adoption, purchase and/or usage.

4.1.3 Communicate trust

To create the awareness needed, and to allow existing customers to transfer the trust they build in the product or brand. Trust is an intangible element in the business process, and as such, there is not a definitive set of steps that will generate, maintain or recover trust.

4.1.3.1 CSR policy

Corporate Social Responsibility (CSR) is vital to the operation of free markets and capitalism today. If our economic system is to flourish, we need to find a way of harnessing ethical entrepreneurship flair in business leaders and the analysts they report to. This is the view of a 2005 Sunday Times report[cxxvii].

CSR has been criticised earlier in this book, as a cheap trick to con the market into thinking a company is trustworthy. Ethical companies, however, do take CSR a step or two further. CSR is more than recycling rubbish, turning lights off and contributing to charity, and many companies have found their programme provides a valuable management tool.

Charity involvement within CSR programmes can include the donation of labour. For example, a team of graduate managers could be sent to help build needed facilities in a developing country to help a charity achieve its targets, and helping the company build teamwork amongst the trainees.

The London Stock Exchange have started to identify the importance of CSR by setting up the FSTE4Good Index, which measures the performance of companies that meet globally recognised corporate responsibility standards, and to facilitate investment in those companies. Transparent management and criteria alongside the FTSE brand make FTSE4Good the index of choice for the creation of Socially Responsible Investment products.

The FTSE4Good has ten declared sets of principles, three of which are 'governmental' and seven of which were created by either Non-Governmental Organisations (NGOs) or business organisations. All have a growing credibility gained from extensive international consultation. These principles were used to create the FTSE4Good selection criteria.

Governmental Principles:

1. Universal Declaration of Human Rights
2. The OECD Guidelines for Multinational Enterprises
3. The UN Global Compact

NGO/Business Principles:

4. CERES (Coalition for Environmentally Responsible Economies)
5. Amnesty International Human Rights Principles for Companies
6. The Caux Round Table Principles for Business
7. The Global Sullivan Principles
8. Ethical Trading Initiative
9. SA 8000
10. Global Reporting Initiative Sustainability Guidelines[cxxviii]

Companies that live to the restrictions a socially responsible, whether legislative or self-imposed, should be applauded, and in turn deserve the respect of their customers. Unfortunately many companies only pay CSR lip service, in the attempt and hope that they will win the admiration and trust of their customers.

4.1.3.2 Ethics

Ethical planning involves running such tests as the Morning Paper test (i.e. what would this look like in tomorrow morning's papers? This is a similar concept to the TV test). When planning an ethical campaign, the ethics of the region or country must be taken in to account. This means that you may plan a highly sanitised campaign so that it can be run in a number of regions or countries, or, alternatively, that the life and scope of the campaign are limited to those areas identified in the planning documentation.

The ideal would be to use the full creative and innovative scope available to you when planning a campaign and limiting it, from the start, to a specific region. This, of course, can be expensive, as each region would require a different campaign. In light of this, as in most business decisions, one should attempt to find the common ground to make use of as many common factors as possible. It may be that each region does have it is own campaign, but economies of scale are exploited by reusing the images, strap lines, etc.

Many advertising campaigns are, unfortunately looked at sceptically by customers, thanks to a history of untruthful and misrepresented claims by some companies, though thankfully this is not a regular occurrence.

Vince Packard saw advertising, PR, politics, etc., manipulating psychological techniques to achieve their goals.

> *… many of us are being influenced and manipulated – far more than we realise – in patterns of our everyday lives. Large-scale efforts are being made, often with impressive success, to channel our unthinkable habits, our purchasing decisions, and our thought processes by the use of insights gained from psychiatry and the social sciences. Typically these efforts take place beneath our level of awareness, so that the appeals which move us are often, in a sense, 'hidden'.[cxxix]*

If we attempt to undertake ethical marketing, we first have to overcome this negative attitude. In an online world, with the wealth of information we can gather from the online habits of our customers, we have the opportunity to scare our customers if we are not careful about the employment and engagement of the knowledge of their behaviour and the techniques at the disposal of modern marketers.

4.1.4   Objectives

One of the important factors in planning a campaign is to define the objectives of the campaign from the outset. If the objectives of the campaign are clear, it is easier to develop the creatives, copy and actions of the campaign.

If the campaign is only a communication, such as an e-mail marketing campaign, it can do the following:

- Convey information
- Alter perceptions or attitudes
- Create desires
- Establish connections between products
- Direct actions
- Provide reassurance
- Remind
- Give reasons for buying
- Demonstrate[cxxx]

4.1.4.1 Objective setting

Setting objectives appears easy. The question that needs answering is 'What outcome do you want?'

The objectives should be SMART - Specific, Measurable, Achievable, Realistic, and Timed.

- **Specific** - Be precise about what you are going to achieve
- **Measurable -** Quantify you objectives
- **Achievable** - Are you attempting too much?
- **Realistic** - Do you have the resource to make the objective happen (men, money, machines, materials, minutes)?
- **Timed** - State when you will achieve the objective (within a month? By February 2010?)

Ten steps to SMART objectives:

1. Sort out the difference between objectives and aims, goals and/or targets before you start. Aims and goals, etc relate to your aspirations objectives are your battle-plan. Set as many objectives as you need for success

2. SMART stands for Specific, Measurable, Achievable, Realistic and Timely

3. Do not try to use that order - M-A/R-S-T is often the best way to write objectives

4. Measurable is the most important consideration. You will know that you have achieved your objective, because here is the evidence. Make sure you state how you will record your success

5. Achievable is linked to measurable. Usually, there is no point in starting a job you know you cannot finish, or one where you cannot tell if/when you have finished it
   How can I decide if it is achievable?
   - you know it is measurable
   - others have done it successfully (before you, or somewhere else)
   - it is theoretically possible (i.e. clearly not 'not achievable')
   - you have the necessary resources, or at least a realistic chance of getting them
   - you have assessed the limitations

6. If it is achievable, it may not be realistic. If it isn't realistic, it's not achievable. You need to know:
   - who is going to do it?
   - do they have (or get) the skills to do a good job?
   - where is the money coming from?
   - who is responsible?
   Realistic is about human resources/time/money/opportunity

7. The main reason it is achievable but not realistic is that it is not a high priority. Often something else needs to be done first, before you will succeed
If so, set up two (or more) objectives in priority order

8. The devil is in the specific detail. You will know your objective is specific enough if:
   - everyone who is involved knows that it includes them specifically
   - everyone involved can understand it
   - your objective is free from jargon
   - you have defined all your terms
   - you have used only appropriate language

9. Timely means setting deadlines. You must include one; otherwise your objective is not measurable. But your deadlines must be realistic, or the task is not achievable. T must be M, and R, and S without these your objective can't be top-priority

It is worth this effort! You'll know you've done your job well, and so will others[cxxxi]

4.1.4.2 Reality checking

It is one thing to develop some SMART objectives that work for the product or service, that work well on the media chosen, but if the campaign requires the customer to do something to make it a success, it may fail.

In the electronic world, the boundaries of reality are somewhat warped as the technology does drive the boundaries. Unfortunately, not all customers can keep up with the technological advancements, just look at the messy demise of boo.com who were technologically advanced, but well ahead of their time for their customers.

4.2 Databases

When planning digital marketing campaigns, one of the most important elements of the plan I how to use the database of customer data, or how to augment the customer information already in the database.

Most databases are now part of a CRM system, which gather information from all the customer touch-points around the company. There have been many commentators announcing the death of CRM, but in reality, the main problem has been a lack of understanding and poor implementation of the systems. As such, if the databases are to be used in the digital marketing activity, the scope of their use must be defined.

4.2.1 CRM

CRM is the means of forming a lasting relationship with the customer, understanding their needs and applying that understanding in a meaningful and profitable way.

Unfortunately, many companies regard CRM as the means to sell more. This leads many customers to state that they do not want relationships with the company, destroying any opportunities to create that relationship and means that the transaction is a one-off.

Where CRM does work, the data must be recent, the communications to the customer frequent (though not too frequent), must provide both parties with a profitable reason to continue the relationship, and it should build a personable relationship over whatever time period is appropriate.

4.2.1.1 Recency

If you gather customer data, with an opt-in to allow you to sell that data on to third parties – the so-called third party opt-in – the information must come from customers who have been active, or actively contacted over the last 12 months. This is a throwback from the direct mail regulations, and I would argue that it is too long a period for the online market. In dealings with the list management industry, I have proposed the use of six month or 180 day recency as a guideline for e-lists.

4.2.1.2 Frequency

With the global increase in spam, the frequency of communications with customers is vital – too much and your messages will be classed as part of the tidal wave of spam. If, however, you communicate infrequently with your customers, you may lose their interest and loyalty.

One solution may be to ask the customers to select their own frequencies. In some unpublished research I undertook in 2002, customers were quite happy to opt-in to company and third party information for an incentive, and that they were happy to opt for increased message frequencies in exchange for greater incentives.

Is this just bribing the customer, and therefore acting unethically? Not really as the customer is in control of the situation, if the frequency becomes too great, they can stop or reduce the communications. If they want the incentives without compromising their privacy, the same incentives were available to purchase (which also gave the incentive a monetary value), so alternatives were available. In this case both the company and the customer were in a position to profit from the relationship.

4.2.1.3 Monetary value

The monetary value of the relationship is dependant on the relationship being fostered. If the relationship requires a one-off purchase, and that purchase can only ever be a one-off, such as a civil engineering project, the monetary value of the contract is high, but the value of maintaining a relationship may be worthless, for both parties.

On the other hand, Fast Moving Consumer Goods (FMCG) products may have a lower unit value, but a long-term relationship could benefit both parties and the additional income possible from the sale of a third party opt-in list can make such relationships viable.

To make the relationship work, both parties must, however, feel that they are profiting from continuing the association. This is where CRM often fails in its implementation, as many companies feel that the information should show all the cross-sell and up-sell opportunities that must be exploited at once. Many customers, however, will shy away from constant hard-nosed salesmanship, even if it is automated via a website.

4.2.1.4 Personalisation

One of the joys of using a CRM system linked to a website is the fact that the site can be programmed in such a way as to customise the interface for the customer.

This requires a registration and login, and can customise the interface for the customer, delivering the information the customer wants, and the messages the company want to convey.

4.2.1.4.1 Intrusion

Personalisation is fine as a means to get closer to the customer, but it does require either that the customer can be bothered to customise their own interface, or that the company holds sufficient, and the correct information on the customer. If not, the personalisation may be seen as an intrusion.

I have often been told that customers do not want a relationship with a company who are trying, at time very hard, to establish a false relationship with them. This hollow interaction is often because of a lack of passion about the products or services being offered, and a lack of sufficient information about the customer.

4.2.2 Relationships/friendships

When I was a salesman, my boss always used to quote that people bought from their friends. When I present this, I add hat I have yet to find a salesperson that I feel is a friend – not whilst they are trying to sell me something!

The concept is, however, correct, in that friendship requires an element of trust, and therefore is a means to building a relationship. Indeed as a Danish proverb notes, *"Distrust is poison to friendship."*

In the modern age, were we have replaced the face-to-face salesmanship with automated relationship software, namely CRM, we are in danger of losing the friendship from the sales process, and hence losing the trust.

As indicated in the previous chapters, trust is an important foundation to loyalty, and the relationship will therefore suffer if this trust is lost. The trust focused value chain (Figure 21) shows that the lack of trust will impact profit, because if being trustworthy is profitable the reverse is also true.

4.2.2.1 Opt-in

One of the means of building a relationship is to have a dialogue with your customers, whether you are automating this with sophisticated software, or employing the human touch. This does, however, require the customer's permission to have a dialogue with them.

Since the Data Protection Act was tightened up in 1998, companies must now obtain the active opt-in to talk to their customers. This can cause a problem for companies that need to cold call customers. But is cold calling any use? The McGraw-Hill advert of the 1970's is a great example of why cold calling is wasted effort (see Figure 27).

Figure 27. McGraw-Hill 'Man in Chair' Advert[cxxxii]

It is important that a company can conduct a dialogue with its customers, to build the trusting relationship. This means that one of the overriding objectives of any digital marketing should be to engage the customer and to encourage their active opt-in.

It is possible to encourage customers to opt-in, in exchange for products or services, but it could be argued that such a relationship is built on the desire or need for the service rather than he seed of a trusting relationship.

In defence of this approach, however, it is only with an open dialogue with the customer, that a company can even start to demonstrate its trustworthiness, irrespective of the methods employed to initiate the dialogue in the first place.

4.3   7P's

Part of the planning process must examine the marketing mix, and the impact it has on the ethical standpoint of the company. A company could, for example, run the most ethical promotional programme for the most unethical, deadly product in the world. Obviously, in such as situation, the efforts made to make the promotion ethical may be wasted.

The 7P's are: Product (or service); Price; Place (or distribution); Promotion; People; Processes and Physical evidence.

4.3.1 Product

4.3.1.1 Policies

Ethical product policies are obviously the most important element of the ethical marketing process, as without ethical products, it is unlikely that a company can create an ethical marketing strategy.

In terms of digital marketing, the speed of delivery is the major benefit that the customers appreciate from the media. But a company can also use the medium to research, develop and test their new product ideas to ensure a beneficial and functional fit with the customer's requirements, even if the customers do not yet know their requirements.

4.3.1.2 Quality

When the ISO9000 quality standard first appeared in the business community, there was a rush by companies to get registered. Many companies thought that a quality standard would demonstrate that their products or services were of merchantable quality, and likewise, customers thought the standard meant the products were of high quality. This unfortunately was not the case.

In this standard, companies set their processes into a set of guidelines that they were then required to follow. This meant that a company could operate unethically, producing shoddy goods, so long as their quality standard guidelines were met.

In such a case, the ethical approach would be to ensure that the quality standards are open for customer scrutiny, and indeed that they are developed with customer involvement. Customers can, after all, accept lower quality if they receive the benefit of lower prices, for example.

4.3.1.3 Lifetime

The product lifetime can be a critical factor in ethical marketing planning. I was shocked in a previous job to find out that professional power tools were designed for a lifetime measured in hours, albeit about 1,500. Do It Yourself (DIY) power tools, however, are only designed for about 10 hours. I thought this was highly unethical at first.

Of course, 1,500 hours of professional use equates to between one and three years of usage. Ten hours of DIY usage, however, equates to about five to ten years, as it is unlikely that an amateur will use a drill, for example, for more than a single hole at a time, so about 45 seconds. Therefore, the difference in lifetime is acceptable, and the DIY product being a fraction of the professional tool price provides the customer with the necessary trade off.

Ethically speaking, though, a product should last a reasonable time before it requires repair or replacement, and the period should be determined by the price charged to some extent. Obviously, heavily branded products are likely to be more expensive than unbranded products, even if they come from the same factory production line.

Artificial retirement or obsolescence of products can be seen as unethical, and the computer industry must be put forward as operating such practices – how often do you need to upgrade a number of software packages because they are no longer compatible with other software.

4.3.2 Pricing

Pricing is a tricky subject. Many customers will see pricing as the most ethically orientated element of the whole marketing mix, often complaining of a lack of value for money, or extortionate pricing.

4.3.2.1 Cost Leadership

Companies occupying what Michael Porter identified as cost leadership need not be acting unethically. Their products may be manufactured ethically, perhaps in low cost locations, but the savings are passed on to the customer.

Exploitation of low production costs normally involves companies manufacturing in locations where wages and regulations are low, and the products are still sold for inflated prices in the richer market places. Practices like these were exposed by Naomi Klein in her book No Logo, with the focus appearing to be the sports equipment manufacturer, Nike.

4.3.2.2 Value for Money

When speaking to customers, both consumer and business, they always indicate a desire to get value for money. The value issue is often thought to be part of the ethical debate, but in reality, there are many intangible factors that add to the value of a product or service that are difficult to quantify.

This is the area where branding and loyalty can build profit, as the demand outstrips the supply. Many luxury brands operate in this way. Unfortunately, if the price exceeds the notional value, the customers will feel let down, and feel that the company is just exploiting the market.

4.3.2.3 Luxury/ exploitation

Pricing can give products credibility. Who would trust a Rolex that cost pennies? Some brands, particularly the luxury labels, have built an intangible desire amongst their customers, and aspiring customers. Earlier in this chapter we identified that some customers aspire to products and services that they do not need or cannot afford. In this case, the aspiration of owning a Ferrari or Rolex watch drives the value of these products higher.

Using the professional power tool example again, some years ago a supplier of such products launched a professional power tool at consumer prices. The product was built to professional standards, albeit a lower end standard, but priced wrongly for the marketplace. As a result, it failed in the marketplace and had to relaunched as a business tool, appropriately priced.

4.3.3 Promotion

Most of this book relates to promotion, in an electronic environment. Promotion is the best means to communicate the ethical standpoint of a company and build the necessary trust in its products and services.

I hope that as this chapter develops, you realise that it is not only about promotion alone, but that the whole marketing mix is involved, and indeed must be involved, as customer see the company through the products or services bring offered.

4.3.3.1 Truthful advertising

What is the difference between unethical and ethical advertising? Unethical advertising uses falsehoods to deceive the public; ethical advertising uses truth to deceive the public[cxxxiii].

Advertising is used to build impressions of a product or service, to inspire or motivate customers. As such, advertising can build a series of false images – the spin that has dogged UK politics during the early 2000's.

Companies that undertake truthful advertising, probably lose out in terms of the WOW! factor, but it does build a longer-term relationship with the customer, and probably one that is more robust.

In the 1990 film, Crazy People, Dudley Moore plays an advertising executive who has a nervous breakdown, leading to a spell in a mental hospital. During this time, he discovers that the inmates were very creative with truthful advertising, such as "you can't get laid in a Porsche, you laid when you get out!" In the film, the extremely truthful advertising message sweeps the US. But why should this be the subject of a comedy film, and not the reality of the market place. Stefansson's quote highlights part of the reason, and another quote, this time from Bill Cosby, the US comedian completes the picture. *"The very first law in advertising is to avoid the concrete promise and cultivate the delightfully vague[cxxxiv]."*

4.3.3.2 Media Selection

The media used to deliver the message is very important. To assume that all customers are connected to the Internet and regularly check their e-mail is a misconception. However, if your business proposition is online only, it may be appropriate to limit yourself to a single media.

I am a great believer in integrated marketing as the ideal approach to the marketplace. In this way, messages are unlikely to contradict one another, and the customer will build a single view of the brand, product or service.

The selection of the media can also promote the trustworthiness of a campaign or company. Generally, e-mails have been driven to a position in which they compete with the porn sites, prescription drug offers and loans or 419 scams. Whilst actively opted in lists can be used, we are fighting the increasing noise. Customers recognise that e-mail is a cheap advertising option, hence the spam problem.

If we adopt an integrated approach, whereby a message is delivered, say in a personalised letter, with a high quality brochure, the customer will perceive the message as being more valuable and more likely to be truthful, trustworthy and hence, ethical (assuming they believe the message itself, of course). If this is then backed up by electronic means, such as a branded and consistent e-mail and a website that reinforces the message, it is more likely to succeed.

If your business model is virtual, then it maybe that no hard copy is required, but, any e-mail communication should be supported by a consistent and complementary website. In almost all cases, e-mails should contain the teaser that encourages the customers to the website.

4.3.3.3 Message Selection

As has been pointed out, the message should be consistent, truthful, and in true marketing communications style – impactful. Some agencies and companies appear to have a problem combining the impact with the truthful and consistent. This only leads customers to distrust the brand or product, through a sense of confusion.

In e-media terms, messages should be concise, and according to the web guru, Jakob Nielsen, the content should be written in an inverted pyramid style[cxxxv], which puts the headlines first, then summarises the content before delving into the details. It must be remembered that web users seldom read copy on the web (though many do print articles off to read later), and that any messages displayed either on a website or e-mail should be easily scannable.

4.3.4 Place (Distribution)

Distribution is often associated with physical marketing, but in an electronic market, delivery can still be possible. If your products or services are virtual, then the web is the ideal delivery mechanism.

4.3.4.1 Availability

The Internet has provided a 24 hour shop interface in which customers can research, order and buy any products or services offered at any time of day, any day of the week, etc, and with the advent of improved mobile computing and telephony technology, from almost anywhere.

As a result of this, and the expectation that conducting business online is faster, products and services are expected to be available at all times, and deliverable in a very short space of time. Indeed the attention span of an average surfer is sometimes, sarcastically said to mirror the memory span of a goldfish, and therefore you only have 7 seconds to grab their attention. In a similar vein, the delivery of some products has to be instantaneous else the customer is lost.

If you order a product from Amazon, they tell you what the availability of that product is – can it be dispatched within the next 24 hours, or do they have to order a quantity in? This is a case of managing the customer's perceptions. In Amazon's case, customers acknowledge that they are buying a physical product that, short of suddenly inventing a Star Trek-like tele-transporter system, will take some time to arrive.

In the case of, for example, ringtones for mobile phones, once an order has been placed, whether this is online or via WAP or SMS, the customer expects immediate delivery of the product. Any delay is likely to infuriate the customer and start to erode the loyalty of the customer.

4.3.5 People

It is one thing to have the trust of your customers, but as a company you also need your employees to trust that you are doing the right thing for them, on their behalf and in their name. If employees feel that they are properly informed and sufficiently empowered, they will act in a similar way to customers, building the trust within the customer base and beyond.

In terms of ethics, many companies claim to be ethical, but employees often think differently. An employee will see all the warts in a company and its dealings with it various publics. In such cases, it could also be said that the employees are part of the company and that unethical practice just mirrors the unethical stance of some employees – how many employees 'borrow' stationery, take longer lunch breaks or fiddle their expenses? Is that not unethical?

4.3.5.1 Beliefs

The beliefs of the employees and customers are a foundation for the ethical standpoint of the company and the ethical framework to which they must perform.

In internationally active companies, the ethical beliefs of the employees will differ from one country or region to another. Customers are relatively static, so the company should only have to been seen adhering to those standards (obviously this is multiplied by the number of markets. In terms of employees, however, they are in a position to see the possible contradiction between approaches, and may feel confused and even threatened by this, if they fail to understand the reasons for it.

4.3.6 Processes

All modern business runs on a series of complex processes. It is possible that these processes come in conflict with the ethical framework of a country or region, although they can equally be developed to augment and adhere to the framework, even multiple ethical guidelines.

4.3.7 Positioning

In ethical terms, the positioning of a brand and product/service, should always be beyond approach. Even for risky products, by attracting the correct customers and addressing them correctly, you can position yourself as operating ethically.

Use of the correct, appropriate media will also help position your proposition, building a trusting relationship with the customers. In terms of a risky product, it may be that it can never be pushed into the mainstream market by your brand, and that unless someone else markets it in the main marketplace, it will remain niche. An example of this is the adult toy market. Ann Summers has brought the products into the high street, leading brands such as Boots The Chemist to look into supplying adult toys.

# 5.	Creatives

5.1 Content

It is often thought that developing innovative or creative campaigns or products can be stifled by the need to adhere to guidelines and regulations. This is not the case. The recent Disability Discrimination Act (DDA) was though to be a barrier to creativity in web design, but it has brought about a new breed of web designs developing in a more user-friendly way, but without any impact on creativity. In fact, creativity has probably been boosted.

Companies can use content to deliver creative messages to customers to demonstrate ethical standpoints and build trust. This can be done two ways, by creative, accurate copywriting, and by using consistent language across all communications media.

5.1.1 Copywriting

5.1.1.1 Techniques

Jakob Nielsen, the web guru has undertaken research to explore how people read electronic media. As such, he has concluded that few people actually read online, although there could be a technological reason for this[cxxxvi].

Nielsen advocates an inverse pyramid style of writing for the electronic media, which is a journalistic style of writing, which also embraces liberal use of list and bulleted lists that facilitate easy scanning.

5.1.1.2 Considerations

All of this sounds great, but if you are limiting copywriters to journalistic styles with lists of attributes or benefits, you may be affecting the creativity. Nielsen's research is important, but should not be the concrete guidelines to e-media development.

Use the research findings as a guide, to temper the development of content and the layout. By doing this, it is more likely that a company will benefit greatly from a greater comprehension by the customer. If the communications are easier to understand, the communication of ethics and trustworthiness should be more forthright and approachable.

5.1.1.3 Typography

Typography can make a message stand out, and it can hide the message. Careful use of typography can enhance the message and the impression that you are portraying.

Using typefaces that are easy to read demonstrate an openness that can, if it matches the message, build on the trustworthiness of the brand or product. If an illegible typeface is chosen, it tends to hide some of the intent, and on a medium that must capture the interest and imagination of its customers in a very short space of time, may well be counter-productive.

Typography is not only limited the choice of typeface, it also includes the layout of text and graphics. To an extent this is guided by Nielsen's research in that graphics can help lead the eye to relevant content. Following the implementation of the DDA, it is not only the visible layout, but now also includes the structural development of websites and e-mail marketing programmes, where tables should be constructed in a particular way, and images should all be tagged with a coded title.

5.1.2 Language

The Plain English Campaign is an advocate for simplifying the language used in all customer communications. This now includes electronic media, and it's over emphasis on jargon.

America On-line (AOL), the internet service provider have conducted a survey into customers' understanding of technical jargon, or 'geek-speak', used to 'advise' internet users about protecting their machines from viruses. Many home computer users have complained of feeling confused and vulnerable due to the fact that often they have no idea what they are meant to be doing. They also do not understand what they are meant to be protecting their machines from.

According to the survey,

- 84% of home Internet users do not understand the term 'phishing', which describes e-mail 'scams'
- 83% of respondents worry about their personal details falling into the wrong hands on-line
- 76% are concerned about unwanted junk e-mail, yet 16% have never heard the term 'spam'
- More than 20% do not know how to tackle on-line risks

Words like 'Trojan', 'Keylogging', 'Spyware' and 'Pharming' (luring Internet users from legitimate to fake websites) are sailing over anxious users' heads as they fight to protect themselves and their machines from criminals.

Given that most computer-related language is inevitably difficult, it seems, even to us, that some of these new 'slang' terms could be useful to non-technical users. However, it appears not enough is being done to publicise the potential dangers of Internet use[cxxxvii].

5.1.2.1 Consistency

The language used in all marketing communications should be consistent across all media communications, with an emphasis on the message, rather than the actual content used. The content should, of course, be consistent, but it must be recognised that different media require different writing styles and techniques.

E-mail campaigns often try to convey too much information, leading to customers deleting the message. Too little information, however, can have the same effect, with customers expected to link to the Internet to read more. Would you expect a customer to pick up a phone or log onto the Internet if as little information is provided in a postal mailing?

5.1.2.2 Tonality

The tone of voice used in marketing communications and product collateral is vital, as all to often, companies talk to their public in a number of different ways, all communicating essentially the same message. This just adds to the confusion and is likely to be a trustbuster.

Whilst the actual content may differ from one medium to another, the tone of voice must remain consistent, reinforcing the brand or product image. It is possible to ensure that the tonality is consistent, even when the media requirements are so totally different.

5.1.2.3 Use of Jargon

Jargon is often said to be a tactic used by insecure employees or industries to increase their importance. Unfortunately, within a business, jargon starts to become commonplace and is used increasingly outside the company.

Working in the Internet and telecommunications industries, I find that jargon is an everyday element of our business. When we deal with suppliers, we can often confuse them with use of the common jargon, and there is often a danger that we push that further to the customers themselves.

5.2 Graphics

Graphics and images can have a great impact on the ethical position of a company. It is not only the use of 'pin-up' images in corporate calendars and trade advertising (and indeed for exhibition personnel), but related concerns may apply to the use of distressing images by charities.

In 1990, the RSPCA (Royal Society for the Protection of Cruelty to Animals) ran an advert to highlight the cruelty of the British Government's policy allowing the live export of ponies and horses to continental Europe for slaughter. The advert, pictured in Figure 28, shows a dead pony hanging on a meat hook.

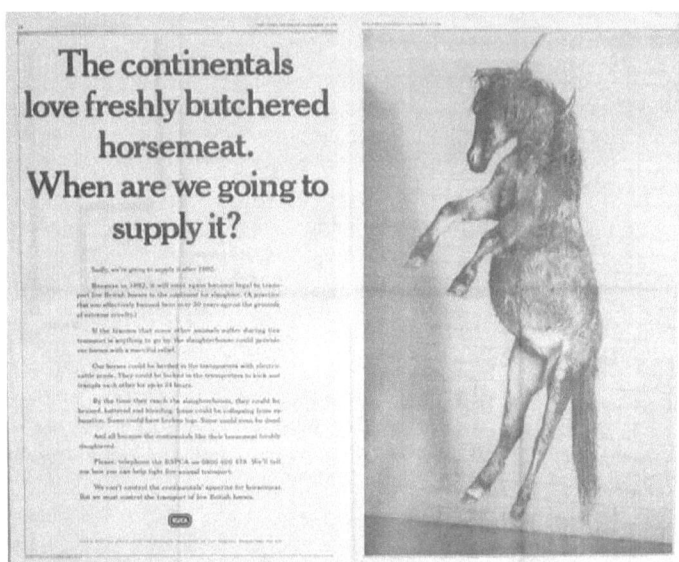

Figure 28. The RSPCA 'Dead Pony' advert[cxxxviii]

The RSPCA were heavily criticised for running this advert, deemed too offensive and contravened the British code of advertising practice. Whilst the public were shocked and outraged by the image, and the RSPCA ordered to issue an apology, the advert did start the debate, presumably fulfilling its objectives.

Alternatively, some adverts can be seen as offensive to a section of the community, or particular religious groups. One example would be the advertising using scantily clad women.

A famous example of advertising using female models is the Wonderbra advertisement whose product targeted women, but advertisement appeared to target men, shown in Figure 29. The product was successful, and the advert famous for launching the career of Eva Herzigovina. Women's groups objected to the imagery and context of the advert, whilst men's groups complained that a billboard version of the advert contributed to an increase in car accidents at a major London road junction! From a marketing perspective, the campaign worked – people still talk about it.

Figure 29. The infamous Wonderbra advert

5.2.1 Consistency

The imagery used in all communications should be consistent in the same way that the content should remain consistent with the message. In terms of the RSPCA advert, had they used the Internet in 1990, their online imagery should have been as graphic and powerful as the print advertising.

Consistency in imagery includes the use of colours. Obviously some media, such as some print media are limited to monochrome presentations, but the imagery should still appear to mimic the different colours used on other media. Shades of colour are just as important to get right, especially now that phishing practices on the web (fraudulently claiming to be a bank or investment company to drive customers to a website to capture their passwords) are on the increase and can often use the wrong colour shades, etc.

5.3 Trust building campaigns

Campaigns that set out to build trust are often cynically put down as a cheap attempt to hide other activities. This scepticism means that it is very difficult to make trust building the main objective of a campaign.

As a result, businesses must look to being open and honest about the messages they do convey to the marketplace, with the trust objective taking second place. This means that if a company has had problems, part of the message should include an apology and a measurable commitment to improve the product or service.

Going the extra distance to please the customer can often buy their loyalty, so gifts and exclusive offers can have a short-term effect, but if the act of giving these gifts and offers is seen as genuine, they can help build a trusting, long-term loyalty.

It has been shown that the active opt-in is not only a legal requirement but also a trust building tool. It is only with this opt-in that you can conduct a meaningful dialogue with your customers. The trust therefore also includes that way you ask your customers to opt-in. There are numerous sites in the US that offer free e-newsletters, but to sign up for them you automatically sign up to receiving any number of third party mailings – there is no opt-out option. When I was confronted by this, I refused to sign up, doing without the e-newsletter I wanted to save my e-mail inbox.

5.3.1 Consistency

One of the most important factors in building trust is the consistency of the message and the service. A customer confronted by a different message each time they are contacted, especially if the messages contradict one another, trust will be eroded, should it have been present at all.

The channels offered to the customer should remain consistent. It may be that as a company you decide that the Internet is the best channel for you to service your customer, but this does not allow you to dictate the switch to the customer, forcing them down a different route.

5.3.2 Keeping promises

Of course one of the vital elements in developing a trust building campaign is to keep the promises you make to the customer. If a customer feels that any promise make by your company is going to be kept, they will come to rely on your integrity.

If you have to make promises constantly due to a failure of your products, you may want to revisit your production policies before continuing with any customer communications. The promises can either be in terms of the product or services offered, or the communications – for example – if you promise to limit your communications to one e-mail per month, then you should stick to that. If you want to change the frequency, it would be better to give the customers an incentive say from the website, to sign up to increased frequencies. In this way, the customer will feel like they remain in control of the relationship.

6.   Media

6.1 Digital Media

Marketing communications is a discipline that covers a large number of media channels, so it seems strange to talk about digital marketing campaigns in isolation. Whilst it is regarded as a separate discipline, we will look at it in some isolation.

In terms of electronic media, we mean websites, e-mail, text (SMS and MMS), and mobile technology (WAP and I-mode). Up and coming marketing opportunities for electronic media are discussed at the end of the book, when we look at the future of digital marketing.

All these media currently rely on telephony of some form to transmit the data, so they have been closely linked to the advances in telecommunications over the last 10 years.

Marketing planning claims to start with thorough analysis of the customers and therefore the marketplace.

Marketing communications (marcoms) strategy is ideally conducted after extensive research and planning. In practice, however, this appears to be a mere aspiration for most marketers. Ethically speaking, this planning is vital to ensure the right message for the right recipient.

Marcoms theory suggests that each campaign needs some stated objectives, normally based on a situation analysis – usually a 'where are we now' position. The target audience should be identified as part of market or market segment, and the campaign message or offer duly positioned to appeal to and address the target segment/s. So far so good.

The fifth century Chinese general, Sun Tzu, is often quoted in marketing and management strategies, and marcoms is no exception. He is credited as identifying the potential barriers to getting messages received and understood (remember the communications model?) – they are:

- **The individual's 'clarity' threshold:** this is the point at which a person sees an event with enough clarity to understand it. When people are confronted with evidence of change, they tend not to take the first input seriously. An example is – 'one cuckoo does not make a spring'
- **The three to five rule:** it usually takes three to five observations before the input is believed. That is, it takes three to five cuckoos to make a spring. If we don't want spring to come, it may take even more cuckoos

- **The preconceived notion:** we have definite opinions as to what to expect, and tend to resist input that opposes our expectations. For example, the radar operators at Pearl Harbour in World War Two expected friendly planes and made that assumption. When we plan an event and believe it is going to work, we can ignore reports of failure. We assign quality factors to incoming information and will reject the information if the sender is unknown

- **The reputation assessment:** our willingness to transmit news depends on our assessment of the reputation of the messenger and how that news affects our personal reputation. Perhaps we prefer to 'shoot the messenger.' Good news travels fast; fast news will be delayed as long as we think the outcome will change

- **The act of communication:** before a message can be sent, it must be formed in the mind of the sender. Quantitative values get in the way. Words such as 'a lot of customers' or 'a variety of lower prices' can have widely different meanings to different people[cxxxix]

Thus, we have to clarify and quantify information – in- and outbound, as described in earlier chapters. Outbound campaigns force customers to look at a message that they may not be interested in – interruption marketing as Godin puts it[cxl]. Inbound messages are initiated by the customer, so there is a higher likelihood that these would be received by the customer.

Goldstein modelled the guidelines for successful digital marketing campaigns as:

- Ask permission. Decide whether to use an opt-in or opt-out question, and then make sure it is clearly and prominently displayed next to your request for an e-mail address. Also think about asking two separate questions – one for your own information and one for third party use

- Identify the source. In every e-mail (& SMS) message you send, use a header that identifies your company as the source – 'This is brought to you as a valued subscriber of X'

- Remember relevancy. Do not waste your customers' time. Send only information you believe will be of interest to them

- Let customers subscribe. At the bottom of each transmission include a footer that allows recipients to remove themselves from your e-mail list, through an e-mail address or unsubscribe URL[cxli]

In previous chapters, we have seen that spammers have certain objectives in their 'campaigns'. This is no different to the objectives that mainstream campaigns should have, but instead of the anti-social and criminal foundation to the objectives, we will be looking to benefit our customers whilst increasing our profits, or brand exposure.

Unethical campaigns often ignore the customer, leading to poorly targeted, ill-received and even unsolicited communications. This then kills the reputation of the messenger - such is the reputation currently of e-mail.

Unethical practice by others can erode, or completely destroy, a channel. This factor has concerned companies such as America Online (AOL), Microsoft and Yahoo! and is being addressed by them in a four-point plan:

- Protect consumers from receiving spam
- Prevent the use of e-mail services to send spam
- Help set up commercial e-mail standards
- Enforce these ideas

E-mail, of course is not the only form of e-media that is affected by spam, but it is the worst affected.

Ethical e-marketers will establish an ethical standard that their customers will accept, respect and ultimately expect from all their suppliers. This must, however be central to all communications, and maintained over time. The ethical position should be clearly stated and communicated to customers, using understandable language that can easily be passed on, giving a viral benefit to the ethical standpoint of the company.

6.2 Websites

In the early days of the Internet, websites were very basic, little more than pages of typed content, with a lack of graphics and very limited reach – few customers were online at the time.

Websites do not have the reputation of being unethical, although many companies now appear to use client-side spyware to 'understand' their customers better. Many web-surfers now employ software that blocks such potentially malicious activities, with the result that any subversive activities are flagged to the customer, with the danger of making them mistrust the vendor/supplier.

When planning a website, as with any other marcoms activity, the objectives of the online presence needs to be formulated. The target audience should be identified and addressed. Remember, even though so many people use the Internet, there are also people with little to no access to the web, and some who have no interest in using the Internet.

A survey in the US showed that approx. 7% of consumers had tried the Internet but turned their back on it because of fear, disillusionment or bad experiences[cxlii]. An integrated communications campaign may try to encourage these customers back to the web, but this may have to be a very specific and highly targeted campaign!

Customers now expect websites to be interactive – the old-days of online reproductions of brochures will no longer do. I remember seeing a brochure that had been scanned and placed on the web by one company in an attempt to have an online presence in the early days! The modern consumer will no longer accept this. Most sites on the Internet today do not focus on building trust as part of an ongoing relationship with their customers[cxliii].

Websites should also be informative – if a customer does not learn anything new from your site, what will entice them to return? As in most areas of marketing, existing customers, even if they haven't actually purchased anything from you, are cheaper converts to your products and services than brand new customers with whom you have had no previous relationship.

The final rule for websites is consistency. Each page on the website should build on the brand identity, the reputation and ethical standpoint being portrayed; even if only slightly. Contradiction is definitely counter-productive. Remember, the website is the company shop-window, every hour of every day of every year!

Urban, *et al*, state that most websites provide consumers with scanty information on which to base their trust. They go on to say that it is no exaggeration to say that as consumers become more sophisticated about the Internet, website trust is going to become a key differentiator that will determine success or failure of many retail web companies[cxliv].

So to summarise the website planning criteria, every website should:

- Have a set of clear objectives
- Target your audience, remembering that some may not be online for some reason
- Ensure the site is interactive
- Make the site informative to encourage the customer to return
- Be consistent with all your offline marcoms activities

This should all be obvious for experienced marketers, but it is important in building an ethical standpoint and therefore a competitive advantage within your marketplace.

Urban[cxlv] cites that trust is a three-stage, cumulative process that establishes 1) trust in the Internet and the specific website; 2) trust in the information displayed and 3) trust in delivery fulfilment and service. They identified the keys to building website trust as:

- Maximise cues that build trust on your website
- Use virtual-advisor technology to gain customer confidence and belief
- Provide unbiased and complete information
- Include competitive products
- Keep your promises

Website trust can also be enhanced by ensuring consumer privacy. But note that building a 'full-trust' website entails big risks – non-competitive products will not survive the process[cxlvi].

A number of commentators asserted that there is a fundamental lack of faith between businesses and consumers on the web and now between businesses, although trust and power emerge as channel partnerships become more dynamic and transitory.

6.2.1 Objectives

The marcoms objectives for a website, whilst building on the company's overall marketing strategy, should make full use of its interactive nature, and its ability to engage the customer at the customer's own pace.

The use of customer databases to store, sort and analyse customer information, and to use that knowledge to deliver personalised information to the customer. This information could be information that fits a profile, or is based on information the customer has requested or provided. This is the basis for CRM programmes, which when properly implemented, can build a business, and generate lasting trust and loyalty amongst customers.

When planning a website, one of the first questions to ask is why do you want the site? Here is a list of possible reasons:

- Everyone else is online
- Customers demand it
- Competitive pressure
- Products and channels are changing
- You need to expand your market reach
- It is an integral part of your company's strategy

The second question prior to building a site is – what do you want your website to do? Sell, build relationships, inform, support, entertain, etc.

If you make your website accessible, easy to follow, you should build the trust and longer term loyalty. If your site appears to be open an honest, there is a good chance that the visitors, and therefore customers, will see it as worthy of their trust.

6.2.2 Design

Website design is a creative activity, and therefore can often be seen as contradictory to analytical processes. This, however, is not really the case, as a carefully planned process will help guide the design.

Web design has now fallen under the control of government regulation, with legislation about the accessibility of sites. The DDA (Disability Discrimination Act) requires that all websites are accessible to all Internet users, including the disabled.

The legislation does not restrict the creative processes, except where bad use of colour combinations are proposed. This, however, should not be seen as a hindrance, as a good designer should avoid these combinations anyway.

6.2.3 Audience

As with all marcoms planning, an understanding of the target audience is vital. The site must be designed with the audience in mind, so a children's site should use simple language, fun graphics and easy navigation. In fact – that is a good formula of all sites, but the language should be adapted to the audience in mind.

It is possible that the targeted audience are overrun by an unexpected influx of customers/visitors, but so long as they enjoy the site as it is, there is little need to alter the strategy.

6.3 E-mail

6.3.1 Objectives

E-mail marketing campaigns should follow the rules that all direct marketing campaigns take. Set the objectives based on the goals of the campaign, using the SMART objectives – Specific, Measurable, Achievable, Relevant and Time based.

The objectives should reflect the media, allowing customers to interact with the message/s, encouraging participation. It should also be noted that any e-mail marketing should first encourage the customer to open the message – this is a problem given the large amount of spam that currently plagues the media. This involves careful wording of the subject line, and for those customers who use the preview pane in their e-mail programme, the first 5-25 lines of the message must tell them who you are, why they should open the message and why they should stay away from the delete button. This is not easy, and may require some trail and error of ideas and methods.

6.3.2 Permission

The key to doing e-mail marketing (and any text marketing for that matter) is to get the invitation of the customer. Under current legislation, this involves getting the customer's active opt-in. Active opt-in means that the customer has physically and actively confirmed that they want information from your company. The older method, and still the common practice in countries such as the USA, is the opt-out. This means that the customer will be assumed to want the information unless they physically confirm they want to opt-out. Unfortunately this sometimes causes a problem as the opt-out can often be hidden.

The permission element of this style of marketing encompasses a great deal of trust, as customers will only opt-in if they trust, or feel that it is possible to trust the company or brand.

You can increase the trustworthiness of your brand image by making the opt-in/-out process very easy to find and understand. Tell the customers how often you plan to e-mail them, and given them options to tell you what information they are or are not interested in. In the research I undertook, we found that customers' trust appeared unaffected by the offer of incentives to opt-in, because they understood that they always had the option to opt-out at anytime.

For the incentive route, we did identify that there may be a group of customers who would exploit our generosity and the legal restrictions to claim the benefits of the incentives but opt-out as soon as they have used the incentive, blocking any communications, only to reapply the following month. In this case, we agreed to block the customers from opting in, as it would be illegal to block them from opting out, of course.

6.3.3 Frequency

Part of the research asked customers on preferred frequency of message, which turned out to be inconclusive. The fact that customers do not actually know what is too high a frequency of messages, demonstrates that relevancy is vital. One wrongly targeted message is too much, and will turn a customer off. Very badly targeted will start to erode, or even destroy the trust. But, well-targeted messages will be welcomed, and frequency is less of an issue.

Part of the research examined the frequency of the communications, and in most cases, again as part of an incentive programme, the customers indicated that they would be prepared to receive more messages in exchange for an incentive. So far so good, but it is all too easy to delete the message whilst still enjoying the incentive. Test, and confirmation e-mails can be used at regular intervals in this situation, to check whether messages are being read. A company must, however, be prepared to remove customers who fail to respond.

6.4 Mobile

Over the last 15 or so years the mobile phone has become commonplace in both business and consumer markets, and is now regarded as a vital business tool. Marketing to mobile phones is now big business, as it is even more direct than e-mail as the phone sits in a pocket or bag, carried everywhere by your customers.

6.4.1 WAP

At the end of the 1990's a new interface was developed for mobile phones, providing them with a similar functionality to an Internet PC. The pages were very low in code and system depth, missing pictures and font variety. This was very similar to the early Internet, and the opportunities offered were almost as big.

Unfortunately at the same time, there was a trend for handsets to miniaturise, making the keypad smaller than previous models, and the screen size reduced accordingly. WAP has proved popular, but not as anticipated in the early days of the technology.

WAP does offer companies an opportunity to provide customers with a means of interacting with customers on a different level, whilst the customer is mobile, and for the right products, it can actually augment the proposition.

6.4.1.1 Objectives

The objectives of a WAP site must first satisfy the product or service peculiarities and the potential customer requirements. For products or services that have little or no mobile potential, a WAP site must be questioned as an extravagant luxury. Having said this, there may be a new opportunity ready to exploit in the mobile area.

The objectives, as with a website, should look at encouraging customers to interact and learn from the company proposition. The site should link the functionality of a web-like interface that customers can trust and interact with, with the benefits of a mobile connection.

6.4.1.2 Content

Not all web content will be applicable to the mobile medium, so you must establish whether the content provides the customer with a benefit, or potential benefit. If this is possible, customers will increase their interaction and increase their loyalty to the company.

In terms of trustworthiness, the increased accessibility to company information can build trust because a company is then open to customer interrogation at any time, from any location – in other words, there is no place to hide.

6.4.1.3 Audience

The WAP audience has traditionally been the younger market, and they tend to be more cynical at first, but then appear to be more loyal and trusting to a brand.

The audience will need to be mobile savvy, but if properly targeted and correctly constructed, it could encourage other customers to use and interact with it. These additional customers must, however, be encouraged to use the interface.

6.4.2 I-mode

I-mode is the Japanese version of WAP, developed around the same time, but this technology has taken the world, especially the Far East by storm. In Europe, an increasing number of mobile phone operators are offering i-mode as a communications tool, increasing its overall reach.

One of the major advantages i-mode enjoys is the open source development platform and profit sharing strategy that DoCoMo, the parent company developed when it launched the technology. It is a secure, lightweight application that provides mobile Internet accessibility from selected handsets.

I-mode has now been withdrawn in the UK due to the strength of WAP, and the growth of smartphones with full Internet browsers.

6.4.2.1 Objectives

Any development objectives for i-mode, would generally mirror those of a WAP portal, in that the relevant content and audience should first be targeted, and the reasons for going online with this mobile technology must be clear.

6.4.2.2 Content

The content can differ slightly from WAP content, as the security on i-mode is regarded as superior, almost to the level of a secure Internet PC. As such, banking operations are very popular, giving customers greater access to their bank accounts in greater detail that ever before.

6.4.2.3 Audience

The audience for i-mode in Europe is predominantly a younger age group, mainly due to the proliferation of games and more youth orientated entertainment. In the Far East, however, a wider range of customers use the medium, giving credence to the development of such technologies as banking interfaces.

6.4.3 SMS

Short Message Services, or SMS developed following a review of the bandwidth usage of mobile phones. It was recognised that a short text messaging service, similar to the old paging services was possible with little to no impact on the quality of voice services on mobile networks. The phenomenal success of the media, especially for peer-to-peer (P2P) communications must have been a surprise to those early pioneers, with an average daily figure of 69 million messages sent in the UK in March 2004, compared with 56 million and 43 million for the corresponding months of 2003 and 2002 respectively[cxlvii].

In the last few years, marketers have identified the potential of SMS as an advertising medium, with direct access to the customer's pocket or handbag. The character restriction, only 160 characters being allowed per message, is not a problem for creative text marketing agencies, and the growth has been astounding.

In terms of direct marketing, SMS marketing offers great opportunities to address the customer directly, in a one-to-one dialogue. Unfortunately, the low-cost nature of digital marketing has attracted at best – lazy marketers; at worst – criminals! SMS marketing has been saved some of the problems of e-mail marketing concerns as it has been a more expensive medium to use, but with prices dropping, SMS spam is a real threat.

As mobile phone handsets become more complex, and the technology improves the communications option, we will see a shift from SMS to MMS that allows the transfer of larger files, with video and audio clips, which offers great opportunities to create impact within the message. Most importantly, MMS offers a means of interactivity straight into a WAP or i-mode site, or in some cases, websites.

SMS spam does not currently have these problems as the operators control the billing for handset-terminated messages. Many spam SMS messages currently ask the recipient to call a premium-rate landline to complete the 'transaction,' so can only really be seen as a hindrance.

6.4.3.1 Objectives

The objectives of an SMS campaign are very similar to any other type of communications campaign, only that the media provides one of the most direct routes to the customer, second only to the traditional face-to-face communications.

Because the media is so very direct, it is also more personal, delivering messages directly to a pocket or handbag, and so any abuse of this media will generate anything from distain and distrust to revulsion from the customer. Text marketers must be more aware of their responsibilities; otherwise the e-mail spam tag will sit firmly with them, possibly killing the medium off. At least with e-mail spam you can filter messages with additional software – mobile phones do not currently have the capacity to add such functionality, allowing all messages through.

6.4.3.2 Content

SMS content is restricted by the character count, but texters have developed their own shorthand which can and has been used by text marketers to make their messages fit, and to appear more acceptable to the texting generation. E-mails can have hyperlinks (click-throughs) to a website or a promotional page; SMS campaigns often point customers to both off- and online touch points.

Legally, each message must have a return address and an option to opt-out from receiving any future messages. This final point is very important – untrustworthy companies are more likely to hide their identities, and prefer not to give customers the option of refusing future communications.

6.4.3.3 Audience

Texting used to be the domain of a young audience. This has gradually expanded to include many older users, though the young are still the largest user group demographically.

An example of an inappropriate campaign target would be an SMS campaign to the elderly. It is true – they may all own mobile phones, but many are unlikely to understand or want to use text messaging (especially the shorthand that is used), and much of the under utilisation of the medium is due to poor eyesight and motor difficulties – the text and keypad cause problems. This is, however, all changing, and the market for this type of direct digital marketing is growing.

If the campaign is appropriate for both audience and message, the audience should – as ever – be segmented, and the message carefully positioned. The copywriting is vital for both media, as they suffer from an immediacy unknown in more traditional channels. A message has to appeal within seconds, or it will be deleted, and the language must be appropriate.

6.4.4 MMS

Multimedia Messaging Service or MMS is a relatively new technology which offers marketers a greater opportunity to interact with their customers, and can therefore help build a better relationship with them.

With MMS, however, most billing packages appear to be based on the data transfer volume, so a spam MMS with a picture, video or audio clip, or worse still, a virus will cost the recipient to receive, as much as the consequences of downloading the message. Ethical campaigns should keep this in mind to avoid being branded as a spammer, time or money waster.

6.4.4.1 Objectives

MMS is similar in its delivery to SMS, but because of its nature – being a medium for pictures, video and audio as well as interactive text, it has a greater scope than its older relative.

The objectives of an MMS campaign should therefore take the characteristics of the media into account, and to make full use of it, to increase the WOW factor for the customers, although as this medium matures the WOW factor will diminish.

6.4.4.2 Contents

MMS contents can include images, video and audio clips to capture the imagination of customers, which allows marketers to build brand images, create awareness and promote trust.

Because of the wide difference in handsets, it is possible that some content or features will not work on certain devices, causing problems with relationships with certain customers. As such, customers should be given the choice of media, just in case certain devices are not compatible – the choice is likely to be a trust-builder.

6.4.4.3 Audience

SMS is seen as a young persons media, and MMS is seen as a more defined version of this. It is of course not true, as many modern phones now have MMS capability, and when activated, it can create a stronger bond with the customers. Some education will of course be necessary for this, which can also help build trust.

6.5 Integrated marcoms

Any marcoms should be complimentary, building on previous campaigns, and making full use of all relevant media. As such, any company with a website should always mix their offline campaigns with complimentary digital marketing campaigns and backed up by the website.

As such, all campaign information should always carry the website address, or link directly to it, use the same images, colours and tonality. In doing this, trust will be built and maintained as the customers acknowledge the brand personality.

6.5.1 Consistency

The key to trust building, integrated marcoms campaigns is consistency. If a series of campaigns retain consistent images, tone of voice, straplines, etc, the customers will be drawn to it, identifying themselves with it longer term.

The company and therefore the marketers, must select a lead medium that will be used as the guide for all the company's communications, and I would argue that this should be the website, as the changes are quick to implement, test and evaluate. Because of this, it is also the cheapest way of controlling the image and the brand.

6.5.2 Objectives

Integrated marcoms campaign objectives are dependent on the objectives of the campaign itself, normally with a lead medium. This means that an offline campaign may take the lead even for subservient messages on other media.

The overriding objectives do, however, have to be consistent with the message and the brand image, building a trusting relationship with the company.

6.5.3 Audience

Integrated campaigns are likely to touch most if not all audiences; although it may be that some campaigns are not appropriate with some customers. An integrated campaign, whilst building the trust and brand character, may not be appropriate in all cases, and therefore some flexibility may be needed in the company's approach.

6.6 e-Commerce

e-Commerce is all about making money, and the internet has proven itself as a great medium for making money. If you think of the e-commerce sites you visit, you will often see a small padlock in the corner of the screen, indicating that the process is secure.

Secure transactions and keeping promises obviously build trust amongst customers, but more striking is the trust-busting character of seemingly insecure sites. Many customers, and I am sure that you are amongst them, would avoid providing their credit card or banking details to a site or through a medium that they deem insecure.

6.6.1 Objectives

Security is one of the overriding objectives for developing an e-commerce interface for their customers. If they can fulfil this, they must ensure that promises made, especially in terms of delivery, are met.

6.6.2 Audience

In most cases, customers who interact with companies via an e-commerce interface will be over 18 years of age, as most transactions are conducted by credit card, and the terms of the credit agreements mean that the customer must be over 18 to initiate the transaction.

This of course does not exclude the option of addressing a younger audience to make use of the 'pester-power' element of children, although the ethical position is dangerous.

6.6.3 Security

e-Commerce relies on appropriate and visible security. Any site that asks for financial information, but fails to address the security issues, will find customers hesitant of transacting with them, and a probably knock-on effect that trust is eroded for the brand and its character.

7.   Delivery

7.1 Electronic delivery

One of the best ways to establish, build and maintain trust amongst customers is to make the promises of delivery of the product or service within a time that is acceptable to the customer, or exceeds their expectations, and then to fulfil that promise.

Many companies make the promises, and build an expectation amongst the customers, but fail to fulfil that promise, letting the customer down and destroying any trust that exists. This failure, may not even be caused by the company, but by a third party, for example a delivery agent who fails to deliver a product, or is inflexible with their delivery service.

7.2 Loyalty

Keeping promises and delivery to customer expectations can build on customer loyalty. This is something that can be seen in Amazon's approach to their market, where they realised that it was not just the online shopping that created trust and loyalty, but to control and own the logistical chain to enable the company to keep their image.

7.3 Channels

When we talk of e-business, we usually also think of the e-delivery channel, which in general is fine for logical or digital products (downloads of various types), but may also involve a mix of on and offline.

In terms of building trust, certain channels may help build more trust than others, as some may be seen as more ethical. The main concern must, however, be to keep the promises to the customer, and as such the chosen channel must be in keeping with the objectives of the company's ethical and logistical strategy.

7.4 Timing

For some products or services there may be a long time lag between the order being placed and the delivery, taking place. This of course, is more likely in the event of a physical delivery.

The most important factor is to keep the promises made to the customer. If the customer is told that the lead time is, say six months, and they are kept regularly updated, trust is often built to a greater level than if the product were delivered immediately.

It is also important to deliver what has been ordered. In the case of Dell Computers, customers are invited to build the specifications of their own PC, laptop or server with some online tools. If the product delivered meets the customers' expectations, it has succeeded, but it does rely on the customer understanding the terminology and technology, otherwise Dell can deliver the correct order, but due to a misunderstanding, the customer does not receive the product they expected.

On the other hand, Tesco (and the other UK supermarkets) have had bad press from their online ordering, home delivery service, mainly in the product replacement sector, where they promise to replace the ordered product, if out of stock, with a similar product. Unfortunately, this has resulted in orders such as 'lemons' being replaced by 'lemon fragrance toilet cleaner', obviously too remote a connection to be of any use to the customer. As a result, many customers felt the service was untrustworthy, but interestingly, they did not associate untrustworthiness of the e-channel with untrustworthiness of the brand as a whole.

8.   Legal

8.1 Legal issues

Direct marketing, with it's 'junk mail' image has been regulated for many years, and this regulation is slowly creeping into digital marketing, though there are issues with regulation of this media thanks to its global nature and the speed of development within the technology.

It is said that the spam is generated by very few 'spam kings', mainly located in the US, Russia and Far East. Surprisingly, legal action is having an effect, as demonstrated by the BBC report:

The net's self-declared spam king is seeking bankruptcy protection.

Scott Richter, the man behind OptInRealBig.com and billions of junk mail messages, said lawsuits had forced the company into Chapter 11 [bankruptcy protection].

OptInRealBig was fighting several legal battles, most notably against Microsoft, which is pushing for millions of dollars in damages.

The company said filing for Chapter 11 would help it try to resolve its legal problems but still keep trading.

Big bill

Listed as the third biggest spammer in the world by junk mail watchdog Spamhaus, OptInRealBig was sued in December 2003 for sending mail messages that violated anti-spam laws.

The lawsuit was brought by Microsoft and New York attorney general Eliot Spitzer who alleged that Mr Richter and his accomplices sent billions of spam messages through 514 compromised net addresses in 35 countries[cxlviii].

The ROKSO List

The Register of Known Spam Operations (ROKSO) database collates information and evidence on known professional spam operations that have been terminated by a minimum of 3 Internet Service Providers for spam offences[cxlix].

Position	Country	Percentage	
1	United States		24.5%
2	China (in. Hong Kong)		22.3%
3	South Korea	9.7%	
4	France	5.0%	
5	Canada	3.0%	
6	Brazil	2.6%	
7	Spain	2.5%	
8	Austria	2.4%	
9	Taiwan	2.1%	
10=	Poland	2.0%	
10=	Japan	2.0%	
12	Germany	1.8%	
	Others	20.3%	

Table 7. The top spam relating countries (as of April 2006)

The main reason for the proliferation of spammers in North America is the traditional lack of regulatory control. The relaying countries are not necessarily the countries of origin of the spam.

The United States continues to lead as the main origin of spam, with nearly 55.7% of all spam being sent from the U.S. In second place we have South Korea (10.2%), followed by China (6.6%); Brazil (3.4%); and Canada (3.1%).

8.2 Data & Contacts

In Europe, privacy is protected by law using the Data Protection Act (DPA) (different names exist throughout the EU). This is designed to safeguard the identity and privacy of the European citizen, and avoid the persecution experienced by some of the population in Europe in the last century. Other countries, most notably the USA, whilst having put formal legislation in place early on, believe largely in self-regulation. Whilst the legislative route is no guarantee against the occurrence of abuse, there is more chance within a system self-regulated by the interested parties and backed up by law.

The Data Protection regulations that came into force in Britain in December 2003 shows the direction the EU is taking with their Data Protection Directive. The focus of the act is to enforce an active and positive opt-in amongst consumers. The rule does not implicitly cover business-to-business (B2B) customers, but I would argue that as these customers are individuals too, and if the details are that of a person (direct dial phone line, personalised e-mail address, etc), then it would be good practice, even ethically sound, to treat them as 'individuals'.

The fact that the regulations only officially relate to business to consumer (B2C) markets is something many commentators and companies seem to forget (or indeed ignore) – business customers are consumers to other companies. Because of this dual role, business customers will become accustomed to the way they are dealt with as a consumer, and may expect this from business contacts – failure to do it may aggravate the relationship despite being legally sound.

8.2.1 Data Protection Act (DPA)

The DPA has altered the face of online marketing, as it has for direct offline marketing and list management in general. The active opt-in required under the DPA has forced many companies to alter their practices. Electronic storage of customer data is also covered, so personal data is protected. Privacy statements, whether on- or offline have all changed to accommodate the changing legislation.

There is as ever, a work around for the tight DPA regulations, allowing a company that has sold a product to a customer to communicate 'similar' products or complementary services they offer to the customer, unless they implicitly opt out. This clause will probably need to be tested in a court of law before we understand the full scope of the legislation. This 'soft' opt-in, as it is called, will provide a lifeline to companies during the transition from an unlegislated landscape to a more stringent environment.

The eight principles of good practice[cl]

Anyone processing personal information must comply with eight enforceable principles of good information handling practice.

These say that data must be:
1. Fairly and lawfully processed
2. Processed for limited purposes
3. Adequate, relevant and not excessive
4. Accurate and up to date
5. Not kept longer than necessary
6. Processed in accordance with the individual's rights
7. Secure
8. Not transferred to countries outside European Economic Area unless country has adequate protection for the individual

The six conditions

At least one of the following conditions must be met for personal information to be considered fairly processed:
1. The individual has consented to the processing
2. Processing is necessary for the performance of a contract with the individual
3. Processing is required under a legal obligation (other than one imposed by the contract)
4. Processing is necessary to protect the vital interests of the individual
5. Processing is necessary to carry out public functions, e.g. administration of justice
6. Processing is necessary in order to pursue the legitimate interests of the data controller or third parties (unless it could unjustifiably prejudice the interests of the individual)

Rights under the Act

There are seven rights under the Data Protection Act.
1. **The right to subject access**
   This allows people to find out what information is held about them on computer and within some manual records.
2. **The right to prevent processing**
   Anyone can ask a data controller not to process information relating to him or her that causes substantial unwarranted damage or distress to them or anyone else.
3. **The right to prevent processing for direct marketing**
   Anyone can ask a data controller not to process information relating to him or her for direct marketing purposes.

4. **Rights in relation to automated decision-taking**
   Individuals have a right to object to decisions made only by automatic means e.g. there is no human involvement.

5. **The right to compensation**
   An individual can claim compensation from a data controller for damage and distress caused by any breach of the act. Compensation for distress alone can only be claimed in limited circumstances.

6. **The right to rectification, blocking, erasure and destruction**
   Individuals can apply to the court to order a data controller to rectify, block or destroy personal details if they are inaccurate or contain expressions of opinion based on inaccurate information.

7. **The right to ask the Commissioner to assess whether the Act has been contravened**
   If someone believes their personal information has not been processed in accordance with the DPA, they can ask the Commissioner to make an assessment. If the Act is found to have been breached and the matter cannot be settled informally, then an enforcement notice may be served on the data controller in question.

Corporate marketing departments have always been hungry for customer data, which the Internet and other electronic media has made easier than ever before to collect. But there are some rules that must be respected in the collection and use of data about customers and visitors to websites. Special attention must, for example, be paid to national data protection regulations and especially to the EU Data Protection Directive 95/46/EC and to the Telecommunications Data Protection Directive 97/66/EC for companies dealing in or with European territories, companies and nationals. Complying with data protection law is a complex process that requires a comprehensive and consistent management approach throughout the whole organisation.

The EU Data Protection Directive was developed to ensure the free flow of data within the European Economic Area (EEA) while safeguarding the fundamental rights and freedoms of individuals. It guarantees the confidentiality of electronic messages and prohibits any kind of interception or surveillance of such electronic messages by any party other than the senders and intended recipients.

According to the directive, member states must determine the conditions under which the processing of personal data is lawful. In any event, the directive provides that personal data can only be collected for 'specified, explicit and legitimate purposes' and must be processed in a way that is compatible with these purposes.

The general rule of complying with e-commerce law is: **be transparent**.

By being completely and fully transparent about who you are, what you are doing and how you will serve your customer, you will find you are not only staying on the right side of the law, but you are also keeping your customers happy. Numerous surveys have shown that customers are not happy with their e-commerce experiences because of a lack of information about what is going on behind the scenes. And in view of the ever-present customer acquisition costs on the web and high churn rates, it only makes sense to keep your customers happy. One way to make them happy is to keep them more information, allowing them to make better decisions.

Personal digital marketing communications under the new regulations can only be conducted when a customer has opted in, and therefore consented to the communications. This therefore means that as unsolicited communications can be sent to them, unless they have given consent to receiving such messages, and the message discloses the identity of the sender. The regulations for digital marketing applies to fax, e-mail, SMS, MMS, voice and answer phone messages.

Personal data can only be collected and processed by the provider if permitted by law or if the individual has unambiguously given their consent – this means the active opt-in.

The points below summarise the main features of the DPA.

Use – Data must not be processed for any purposes incompatible with those for which the data was initially collected. Data cannot be transferred to third parties without agreement from the data subject. Security measures must be taken to protect the personal data against any accidental or unlawful destruction or accidental loss. Data should not be kept longer than necessary for the purpose for which it was collected.

Access – Data should be accurate, complete and kept up-to-date. The customer must have access to any personal data concerning him/her that is being processed or kept. A request for correction or deletion of incorrect personal data must also be granted within a reasonable period. The customer must have the possibility to opt-out of the processing operation of his/her data and to refuse certain use of the data.

The level of security must be appropriate to the risk presented by the nature of the data and by processing it. The individual has the right to object to the processing of personal data relating to them if it is used for the purpose of direct marketing, or if payment systems are not in compliance with data protection principles (specified and lawful purposes, adequate, relevant and not excessive, accurate, securely held, not transferred to third countries without adequate protection, consent).

It should be noted that detecting interception or surveillance is very difficult. However, there are numerous security systems on the market to prevent surveillance. Governments are generally exempt from this barrier, normally in the case of suspected criminal or national security issues.

> **Relevance** – Data should be seen as a perishable commodity and when collected, can and does go out of date. Obviously historic data collected about a person has a longer shelf life than current information, but the data must also be used contextually, which means that the customer will no longer be interested in all products during their lifetime.
>
> An example of this is a pregnant woman who registers onto a 'baby-club' website, getting the benefits of their products and information. Once the child is born, the products and services should change from antenatal to postnatal. If the company owning the information on the 'customer' does not offer postnatal products or services, they cannot pass the information on without the active approval of the individual, nor should they continue sending their information when it loses relevance.

Active opt-in does not just mean ticking a box on a form or website. Taking an action, for example entering an SMS competition, means accepting the terms and conditions and opting in to limited communications. The data, and therefore the opt-in should be time limited – the data has a 'use-by-date' – relating to the relevancy and recency of the information. When selling lists, management companies require that the data is recent; this normally means that it is no more than 12 months old, although different companies may have different timescales.

Legacy is a worry for many companies – for example, utility companies have extensive databases of information on their customers – they are asking whether they must gain the active consent from existing customers to continue sending matching material? The answer is quite complex, but can be summarised by saying NO! There is a provision for a 'soft opt-in' as has been indicated. Soft opt-in means that the customer has initiated the interaction with the company, and it is therefore deemed acceptable to send similar or complementary product information to those customers. There should, however, always be the opportunity for the customer to opt-out at anytime. The sale does not even have to have been completed for the soft opt-in rule to apply, as the indication of interest is sufficient.

Opt-out is an important area on its own, in that every customer should be able to opt-out at any time, free of charge, or at the standard rate for that communication – this means that an SMS opt-out can only be charged at the normal SMS rate, but not at a premium rate. When a customer has opted out, this must be immediate, and without restrictions.

In examining the UK mobile phone market, the author undertook some research on the opt-in and discovered customers were happy to opt-in, in exchange for an incentive. The incentives considered could have been consumed in a matter of hours, although the objective was to encourage a month-long opt-in. If a customer opted in to receive the incentive, used it in a matter of hours or days, and then opted out, the company would have to accept the opt out and suspend all outbound communications to that customer. There would generally be no restriction to that customer opting in again the following month and repeating the process. Whilst accepting this potential problem it was still planned to implement the incentive, and put some trust in our customers. This trust is, however, limited whereby serial abusers of the system will be blocked from opting in, in future – as they could not be blocked from opting out!

An area of profitable activity for many companies over the years has been the sale and management of their 'lists' of customer data and in fact a whole industry of specialist data management companies exist. The new regulations have seriously curtailed the traditional list management activities, but there is still an opportunity to operate lists, within tighter guidelines. Any data collected before the change in the law in December 2003 can be used for company and 'group' use (if applicable), and should always have an opt-out in every message. Data collected since December 2003 must have a demonstrable and active opt-in, contain valid addresses, and it is recommended that it also have an opt-out on each message.

What about new customers, since December 2003? The soft opt-in is still valid for similar transactions, but the regulations go some way to dissuade use of this. It cannot be used for competitions or induced entries, and has the disadvantage that every message must include a simple opt-out.

Disclosure of the identity of the sender is now a 'must' in all commercial communications. The mobile phone company Orange, has invested a great deal of time and effort to minimise the loss of message in their SMS marketing – they start the message with "Orange recommends…" or "Orange offers…". The customer is therefore in no doubt as to who has sent the message. SMS obviously causes a problem as it is limited to 160 characters, and the disclosure has to appear on each message – even if truncated! This is certainly a consideration for any companies with an Internet presence and considering a rebrand, e.g. Abbey National changing to 'Abbey', though I am sure the SMS issue was not a consideration there.

The message must always include a valid postal address, highlight the opt-out procedure, identify the message as an advertisement, who sent the message and provide a return address. The SMS problem is obvious – but for e-marketers, this should be seen as an opportunity to send creatively concise and carefully targeted messages. Service messages to customers are not included in the regulations, but care must be taken not to abuse this by adding advertising in the message body.

Other areas that have been targeted by the regulations include the location-based services (LBS) used on mobile telephones and the use of cookies on websites. LBS technology uses triangulation of telephone masts to pinpoint the mobile phone and to match that to the locality. In this way, a marketer would know that the customer is near their store and, for example, could text them a voucher to encourage them into the outlet – but this still needs the opt-in.

Finally, cookies are bits of Internet code pushed onto a browsing computer by a website to help the site owners recognise returning visitors and record information relevant to the interaction. Cookies improve the customer experience on many websites, but customers must be able to opt-out if necessary without loss of service. If third party cookies are used on the website e.g. by an advertiser, they must also comply fully with the DPA.

8.2.2 Can The Spam

The Controlling the Assault of Non-Solicited Pornography and Marketing Act requires unsolicited commercial e-mail messages to be labelled (though not by a standard method) and to include opt-out instructions and the sender's physical address. It prohibits the use of deceptive subject lines and false headers in such messages. The Federal Trade Commission (FTC) is authorised (but not required) to establish a "do-not-e-mail" registry. State laws that require labels on unsolicited commercial e-mail or prohibit such messages entirely are pre-empted, although provisions merely addressing falsity and deception would remain in place. The CAN-SPAM Act took effect on January 1, 2004[cli].

The law is a pro-consumer measure that allows consumers to choose to stop further unsolicited spam from a sender. It also provides a protection against spam containing unmarked sexually oriented or pornographic material.

Background to this law is:

- **Spam is seen as a problem for Americans**. E-mail is an extremely important and effective means of communications and is used by millions of Americans on a daily basis for personal and commercial purposes. Its convenience and efficiency, however, are increasingly threatened by the rise in spam. Spam currently accounts for over half of all e-mail traffic. Today, most spam is fraudulent or deceptive in nature. The growth in spam also imposes significant costs on Internet Service Providers (ISPs), businesses, and other organisations, since they can only handle a finite volume of e-mail without making further investments in their infrastructure

- **The law provides a well-balanced approach that will help to address some of the harmful impacts of spam.** The problems associated with spam cannot be solved by Federal legislation alone, but will require the development and adoption of new technologies. Nonetheless, the law will help address the problems associated with the rapid growth and abuse of spam. The new law establishes important 'rules of the road' for civil enforcement by the FTC, other Federal agencies, State attorneys general, and ISPs to help curb spam. It also creates new criminal penalties to assist in deterring the most offensive forms of spam, including unmarked sexually oriented messages and e-mails containing fraudulent headers. At the same time, the law caps statutory damages for civil violations in most cases. The law also provides greater certainty in interstate commerce for businesses that would otherwise face a wide diversity of state laws on spam

- **The law builds upon the Administration's efforts to empower consumers with choices in the technology field.** Under the law, consumers are provided with a choice not to receive any further unsolicited messages from a sender. Senders that do not honour a consumer's request are subject to civil penalties

- **The law strengthens a cornerstone of the Administration's agenda to help protect children against pornography.** The law makes spam containing unmarked sexually oriented material a criminal offence. The labelling requirement gives parents a tool to protect their children from such messages. Under the law, senders of e-mail are required to place warning labels on messages containing sexually oriented or pornographic material. If they knowingly violate this requirement, spammers are subject to fines or imprisonment

- **The 'Administration' supports the law's tools to help deter the harmful effects of deceptive and misleading spam.** The law establishes both civil and criminal prohibitions to deter spammers from using false or misleading identification, and imposes penalties against spammers for these violations[clii]

So far so good, but is it working – no, according to NewsTarget:

> Long after passage of the CAN-SPAM Act, spam remains a
> huge problem for e-mail users. It also remains a significant
> annoyance to e-mail marketers who find their messages lost in
> the clutter of spam.

*It's easy to forget that CAN-SPAM was once hyped as the solution that
would end all spam. But that was only the wishful dreaming of
legislators who tend to think that passing laws automatically causes
widespread compliance with those laws. In reality, spammers thumbed
their noses at the law and kept on spamming[cliii].*

8.2.2.1 Compliance

A new study shows that the positive anti-spam effects of CAN-SPAM
legislation were quite brief: while 3% of spam complied with the law
during early 2004, that number has now dropped to 1%. Neither
number is reassuring, and both numbers demonstrate that CAN-SPAM
compliance is fast approaching zero. It's yet more proof that only a
technical solution - like the Puzzle Solution - can bring spam to its
knees.

Essentially, spammers have realised that complying with CAN-SPAM
offers them no benefit. Why should they add the word "ad" to the
subject of all their e-mails when they make more money by leaving it
off? So stopping spammers is an economic issue, and only a technical
solution that changes the economics of spamming practices can alter
the outcome[cliv].

66% of online businesses violate CAN-SPAM, but few send spam –
this was the conclusion of an independent report on the Can-Spam Act
by Arial Software during its first six months[clv].

> *The most relevant finding of this study is that only one-third of
> online businesses send e-mails that are CAN-SPAM compliant.
> The other two-thirds remain in violation of CANSPAM, primarily
> by failing to include unsubscribe links (51%) and failing to
> clearly identify the source of the e-mail (45%). Note that there
> is overlap in these two figures as many organisations fail on
> both counts.*

This level of non-compliance seems surprising, given the widespread publicity of CAN-SPAM and the ease of becoming compliant. On the positive side, even though these businesses do not comply with CAN-SPAM, they almost never engage in spamming. Only three organisations out of 1,057 engaged in e-mail behaviour that most people would consider spamming (high volume commercial e-mails and an unsubscribe function that didn't work), meaning that 99.6% of online organisations don't spam, even when they aren't CAN-SPAM compliant.

CAN-SPAM compliance features

The US legislation known as the CAN-SPAM Act became effective on January 1, 2004. The Act mandates that e-mail marketers comply with a number of specific requirements when sending commercial e-mail. The intent of the law is to curb the sending of fraudulent and misleading commercial e-mail and put in place a single national standard and set of laws for e-mail marketing practices, including unsubscribe processes and advertisement notifications. The following are features that denote compliance with the Act.

Global Unsubscribe:

- Unsubscribe an address from all lists within an account
- Addresses should be manually entered or uploaded in files
- Addresses should also be added to "blacklists" (i.e. suppressed)

Blacklist (suppression):

- To prevent certain e-mails or domains from receiving e-mails from the company - i.e. aol.com
- Applies to all e-mails in an account
- Addresses can remain in the account, but are suppressed

Postal Mailing Address Footer:

- Insert the sender's postal mailing address (as default from company account information) into a "footer"

Unsubscribe - Link or Reply To:

- An unsubscribe message and link should be inserted into all messages. Upon clicking the unsubscribe link, recipients are taken to a profile update page or simple unsubscribe page, where they can opt out of that mailing list

Profile Pages:

CAN-SPAM requires that senders of e-mail enable recipients the option of unsubscribing from individual or multiple lists, as well as opting out of ANY and ALL future e-mails from the sender

8.2.2.2 Risks

The risks for companies trying to compete with businesses that ignore, or worse, abuse the new laws are, thankfully minor, although it does threaten the credibility of online media. NewsTarget anticipate that spammers will continue to outfox all technological advances to eradicate them, so this in itself could kill the media.

If compliance with the law were to be upheld worldwide it would make the eradication of spam easier and more likely. But whilst it is more likely that a compliant company is disadvantaged for remaining legal, legislation such as Can the Spam is unlikely to have much effect.

8.2.2.3 Advantages

For marketers, the most challenging requirement of the new CAN-SPAM Act will be the maintenance of an "Unsubscribe" list of e-mail addresses. Under the CAN-SPAM Act, any time that e-mails are sent by your company or on your behalf, all unsubscribed e-mail addresses must be removed from your list. If, like most marketers, you have many companies who send e-mails on your behalf, you will be required to coordinate with all companies to ensure that an unsubscribed user is never e-mailed to again. This can quickly become a labour-intensive, costly and risky enterprise[clvi].

This is the advice from a company set up to provide support to US companies trying to comply with the law. But as the Arial Software research shows, even apparent compliance is still in breach of the law, and is not being acted upon. As with the DPA, Can the Spam is a good discipline to have, to ensure that customers see the company in a ethical manner, and builds trust with all its stakeholders.

8.2.2.4 Comparisons

The lack of regulatory pressure is probably the most apparent similarity between the DPA and Can the Spam, and there is no incentive for many US companies to adhere to the stricter Safe Harbour regulations, when they see the lack of compliance within the EU.

The list of Known Spam Operations (ROKSO) printed at the beginning of this chapter demonstrates part of the problem with both sets of regulations. Only one operation on the list is from the UK, and some operate out of Russia, China and the Philippines for example, the latter being outside the influence of the regulations, and harnessing the Internet's global reach!

8.3 Disability and accessibility

Accessibility is the degree to which anyone can access and use a website using any web browsing technology.

People with disabilities are a natural audience for the Internet, given its availability and adaptability to assistive technology. According to the National Organisation on Disabilities (www.nod.org), persons with disabilities increased their use of the Internet at twice the rate of people without disabilities (400% versus 200%) between December 1998 and June 2001. The share for persons with disabilities still lags those without (56% versus 38%), but the gap is closing quickly.

A fully accessible site is one that is designed to make use of the latest web technologies such as multimedia, while at the same time accommodating the needs of those who have difficulty with or are unable to use these technologies.

Disability Rates:

Among people with disabilities in the USA:

- About 30% have limitations on their mobility
- 25% have limited use of their hands
- 16% have cognitive impairments
- 13% have impaired hearing
- 12% have visual impairment
- 4% have speech and language impairments[clvii]

In the UK this means:

- 59 million - The approximate population of the United Kingdom[clviii]
- 8.5 million - The number of people with some form of disability in the United Kingdom[clix]
- 2 million - The number of people with sight problems[clx]
- £40-50 billion - The combined estimated spending power of disabled people[clxi]

Under the Disability Discrimination Act 1995 (DDA), a disability is a physical or mental impairment that has a long-term or substantial effect on a person's ability to carry out day-to-day tasks.

This ranges from people with physical and sensory impairments to people with diabetes, disfigurements, heart disease and epilepsy. Not all of these affect how an individual may access the Internet however.

- *Visual* - blindness, low vision, colour-blindness
- *Hearing* - deafness
- *Motor* - inability to use a mouse, slow response time, limited fine motor control
- *Cognitive* - learning disabilities such as dyslexia, distractibility, inability to remember or focus on large amounts of information

Many of these people are, or will be your customers, and just as the Disability Discrimination Act forced company premises to be accessible to all customers through the building of wider door, ramps, induction loops for improved hearing, etc, websites and digital marketing must also make adjustments.

8.3.1 Disability Discrimination Act (DDA)

The Disability Discrimination Act 1995 - (the DDA), was introduced with the intention of comprehensively tackling the discrimination which many disabled people face. The part of the DDA that states websites must be made accessible came into force on 1 October 1999 and the Code of Practice for this section of the Act was published on 27 May 2002.

Disability Discrimination Act (DDA) 1995, Section III

19. - (1) It is unlawful for a provider of services to discriminate against a disabled person-

(a) in refusing to provide, or deliberately not providing, to the disabled person any service which he provides, or is prepared to provide, to members of the public;

(b) in failing to comply with any duty imposed on him by section 21 in circumstances in which the effect of that failure is to make it impossible or unreasonably difficult for the disabled person to make use of any such service;

(c) in the standard of service which he provides to the disabled person or the manner in which he provides it to him; or

(d) in the terms on which he provides a service to the disabled person.

Code of Practice (revised) - Rights of Access Goods, Facilities, Services and premises:

2.17 - It is important to remember that it is the provision of the service which is affected by Part III of the Act and not the nature of the service or business or the type of establishment from which it is provided.

In many cases a service provider is providing a service by a number of different means. In some cases, however, each of those means of service might be regarded as a service in itself and subject to the Act.

8.3.1.1 Compliance

It is critical that websites and web based software be accessible, but the process doesn't have to be difficult or laborious so long as you plan ahead and pay attention to user needs. But why bother?

Websites have to be accessible so that people with visual, hearing, physical or cognitive disabilities are able to take advantage of the information, product, or service you are offering.

If a customer with any form, and any level of disability tries to interact with you using electronic means, and there is no indication of any attempt to facilitate the interaction, it is likely that they will sue under the DDA. Obviously, from a financial and publicity point of view these are undesirable, but from an ethical point of view, a demonstration of how customers are ignored and poorly valued, is an example of poor management and flawed marketing.

Most commentators, however, talk about compliance of websites, indeed there are a number of quality standards now available. Unfortunately, many of the standards organisations are operating a dual role, offering an audit and quality standard on the one hand, and offering consultancy or trying to police the regulations on the other. As a result, I have set up a company called DDA Audit (www.dda-audit.co.uk) to offer an impartial standard, one proving to be very popular in the market.

As this book, hopefully demonstrates, digital marketing is not just about websites, and also involves e-mail marketing, SMS, etc. From an ethical standpoint, these media should be subject to just as stringent assessment as websites.

8.3.1.2 Risks

There are two main risks associated with the development of compliant digital marketing. You could run the risk of alienating the less disabled and 'able-bodied' customers, and you could find yourself in an uncompetitive situation over competitors, especially overseas competitors.

One solution originally touted as a way around the legislation is the development of a text-only version of the marketing. This in itself is automatically discriminatory, and involves twice as much work on the part of the marketers and developers. Both versions must, however, be identical in their content (or description of content) as this again is discriminatory.

As for the competitiveness question, this could be levelled against any work or activity to build a socially responsible image and ethical standpoint within the market. Surely it cannot be an ethically or commercially sound policy to exclude any customers from interacting with the company?

8.3.1.3 Advantages

The risks are very minor, so the question of ethics and commerce asked above is surely one that no company must ask? It should always be the objective of every company to build trust amongst all its customers and prospects.

Compliance is the ethical decision. Supporting web accessibility is simply good business practice. Failing to care for all your customers will cost you in sales and possibly in negative publicity. Accessible web design is an easy way to show that your customers matter to you.

One of the html coding standards being used as part of the accessibility methodology is the use of language tags. In this, the browsers are told which language the content is written in, and in some cases, in which dialect. Should a foreign word then be introduced in the body of the text, a coding tag surrounds the word so that screen readers can acknowledge the change of language. This therefore allows access to a global community of disable customers, not just their able bodied countrymen!

8.3.2 Section508

Section508 requires that US agencies' electronic and information technology is accessible to people with disabilities. The Centre for Information Technology Accommodation (CITA), in the US General Services Administration's Office of Government wide Policy, has been charged with the task of educating Government employees and building the infrastructure necessary to support Section508 implementation[clxii].

Section508 is the US version of the DDA. Unlike the DDA, the standards cover the full range of electronic and information technologies in the Federal sector, including those used for communication, duplication, computing, storage, presentation, control, transport and production. This includes computers, software, networks, peripherals and other types of electronic office equipment.

8.3.2.1 Compliance

As with the DDA in the UK, developers and marketers who work toward web accessibility will discover an immense amount of knowledge dedicated to coding/design techniques. Web pages utilising accessible standards incorporate the best in coding practices and developers may realise an increase in their coding and page development skills. And, of course, the Internet audience will appreciate and benefit from page improvements.

8.3.2.2 Risks

The scale of the disability problem is far greater in the US purely because of the greater number of people in the country, so risks are minimal. There are the same issues as were outlined for DDA compliance, but with the same answers and solutions.

8.3.2.3 Advantages

The advantages of applying the Section508 regulations to the design of any digital marketing is by now, hopefully, obvious, and provides a fantastic foundation to develop other ethical and trust building activities.

8.3.2.4 Comparisons

In terms of e-business, both the DDA and Section508 cover the same ground, and are guided by the World Wide Web Consortium (W3C) and their classification of accessibility. It is, therefore, hardly surprising that W3C are supporting this, given that one of it's directors, and the man attributed with founding the modern Internet, Sir Tim Berners-Lee said, "The power of the Web is in its universality. Access by everyone regardless of disability is an essential aspect."

8.4 Distance selling

Any business operating a system for offering goods or services that consumers can buy from home is affected by the Distance Selling Regulations. The regulations give certain rights to consumers when they shop from home – regardless of whether the shopping is done by phone, mail order, fax, digital television or over the Internet.

There are, however, some exceptions, including business-to-business contracts; financial services; auctions; and contracts for the sale of land. Most of the regulations do not apply to food and drink delivered on regular rounds (for example, a milk round); as well as transport, accommodation, catering or leisure services that are provided on specific dates, timeshare agreements and package holidays.

8.4.1 Compliance

It is important that the company makes sure that it gives consumers the following information in writing before they buy:

- The company name and normally also its address
- A description of the goods and services
- The price – including all taxes
- Arrangements for payment
- Delivery costs if they apply
- Arrangements for the delivery (usually within 30 days unless the contract states otherwise)
- The right to cancel the order (unless there is no such right)
- For long-term contracts, the minimum duration of the contract
- For how long an offer or price is valid

Following the decision to buy, consumers are also entitled to:

- Written confirmation of the information mentioned (except the last two items on the list), unless that information has already been given in writing e.g. in a catalogue
- Details of when and how customers can cancel (including a cooling off period)
- A proper address for complaints (not a PO box number or e-mail address, though these may also be provided)
- Details of after sales services and guarantees
- When and how consumers can terminate any contract that lasts longer than a year or has no specified end date

The regulations also give consumers the unconditional right to cancel an order and any related credit agreement:

- Goods - seven working days, starting from the day after they are received
- Services - seven working days, starting from the day after the contract is made

There are certain types of goods that do not have a cancellation right (for example, personalised goods) and you can prevent a consumer cancelling a service contract once you have started to provide the service. Where a consumer cancels, if they have paid in advance you must refund all the money within 30 days, though you can normally charge them for the cost of returning the goods.

You should also remember that consumers still have their normal statutory rights to return all faulty or misdescribed goods at no charge.

It is an offence to make a demand for payment from consumers for unsolicited goods or services if you do not have cause to believe you have right to payment. Anything unsolicited can normally be treated as a gift and to ask for payment for such products or services will often be a criminal offence.

It must also be noted that any consumers whose credit card is used fraudulently for any type of home shopping can now cancel the payment and the card issuer must refund all the money.

The cooling off period and right to cancel do not apply to contracts for:

- Goods made to the customer's specification
- Perishable goods (flowers, fresh food)
- CD, DVD, and tapes with software, audio or video if unsealed
- Newspapers and magazines

Betting, gaming and lotteries

8.4.2 Risks

The risks to companies relate to interpretation overall, as this example shows:

EasyCar sets their pricing on the level of demand, but in giving users of its "book early pay less" online car rental the right to "cool off" and cancel bookings under distance selling legislation, they felt that their trading strategy was being abused, or had the potential to be abused. The European Courts of Justice ruled that easyCar were not exempt from the distance selling cancellation rights, causing friction with their strategy.

8.4.3 Advantages

By adhering to this consumer-friendly legislation, a company can demonstrate ethical principles and build trust amongst its customers very easily. The requirement to include an address, provide a cooling-off period, etc, are all normally included in most offline business cases (except the easyCar example above), and therefore, this law should be easy to comply with.

8.5 Other considerations

8.5.1 Ethical

As has been shown, earlier in this book, ethics have largely developed from religious teaching, so it is not unusual for companies to fall foul of religious factors. The most recent one has been the opening times of supermarkets over religious holidays such as Christmas and Easter.

We have slowly been eroding the 'day of rest' image of Sunday's with many shops now trading, albeit with slightly reduced opening times. We also have many stores open 24-hours per day, and therefore the amenity of the shop opening times seems to have overridden the 'ethical' debates. This is, however, not a widespread acceptance, with areas such as some Scottish islands trying to retain the sanctity of the Sabbath. I have experienced life in a country where people do not cut their lawns, wash their cars or their clothes, let alone go shopping on Sunday, and any retailer trying to change this may well be seen as acting unethically.

8.5.2 Legal

It is quite likely that the EU will increase the legislation to control and protect the e-media activities of companies and certain individuals. The regulations are, if previous acts are a guide, likely to be far stricter than those that other countries will implement, causing EU companies more problems and cost, but then providing them with a competitive advantage over their international rivals.

The legal assault on spam and illegal activities online will continue, and will, hopefully soon succeed. The EU has done much to prevent this, so we must look at the other nations, most notably the US to tighten up on this.

9.   Action

9.1 Use of interactive media

In a telematic society, each person will have access to several information sources and services on a local, regional, national and worldwide level through the so-called "electronic highways". These huge possibilities do carry certain risks, like the risk of "information overload". There is a risk in diminution of the own problem solving abilities of the individual[clxiii].

The major difference between the new media and the more traditional media is the interactive nature of the channel, which offers great opportunities for marketing. This opportunity covers two areas. The marketer can learn a great deal from the customers through this interaction, and the customers can select the direction the interaction can take place.

9.1.1 Consistency

"Policing the brand," marketing lingo expressing the need to ensure the consistency of a defined corporate identity - a responsibility that the marketing community at large has approached enthusiastically if not with a degree of irreverence - has come under even more scrutiny as recent years have shown businesses big and small trimming their focus to one of improved productivity. With new web technologies constantly appearing, maintaining brand consistency and 'policing' marketing initiatives has proven difficult.

On one hand, web-based tools are empowering; on the other hand, web-based tools are empowering and it is scaring those who have spent considerable financial resources building brands conveying vital messages, targeting specific audiences. The key to any successful marketing execution is the right strategy behind it.

It is thus even more important to identify how to best reach your target audience, and how to use specific elements of interactive marketing to accomplish specific objectives. The focus should develop strategies that take advantage of some of the unique attributes of interactive media:

- Highly targeted unduplicated reach
- Compound branding
- Accountability and the immediacy of data
- Allowing the consumer to control interaction
- Near real time interaction and optimisation
- Relationship marketing efficiencies
- Viral marketing catalyst

Interactive media puts the control in the hands of the consumer, requiring consumer centric strategies. Even a notional control helps the customer build some form of trust with the company. The electronic media offer these opportunities in greater depth than ever before.

Interactive media can accountably shift consumer attitudes as well as drive response, conversion and initiate consumer relationships. The reach and frequency of the media can be predicted and accounted for. More importantly, both behavioural (direct response) and attitudinal (branding) metrics can be monitored, benchmarked and optimised.

It is important to focus on the message and positioning across all collateral, including multimedia presentations. In addition, a comparison of competitive activity is important to develop ones own strategy.

A website can serve as a company's premier marketing tool, a facilitator of direct sales, a technical support mechanism, or it can be used for purposes of public, customer, investor or employee relations.

Internationally, websites are often customised, or localised for foreign markets, taking into account local language or cultural issues, business or social standards and aesthetic preferences. But, depending on the corporate objectives, generally the website should remain consistent across all territories, but the idea of making versions of a site for different cultures implies a desire to show the consumers that the organisation is willing to accommodate their needs. According to recent research, users perceive a company more favourably (for example, more trustworthy, more likeable, etc.) when they see a version of its website in their mother tongue, regardless of the user's English proficiency[clxiv].

From a marketing perspective, brands need to realise that being an international brand means that each section of their target market is as equally important as the home one. German or Polish website users believe that they are entitled to as much attention from a brand as their American or British counterparts, after all they are paying just as much money for the product. At the end of the day it is for the seller to make an effort in a transaction, not the buyer[clxv].

Keep consistency with the company brand. A website developed correctly should permit a viewer to experience the essence or brand that is consistent with the offline company brand.

9.1.2 Integration

Integrated campaigns are the way to build a single, trusted brand image in the marketplace, providing the company with a competitive advantage. An integrated campaign will cover on- and offline media, adapting the interactivity accordingly with the actual media.

9.1.3 Speed of response/action

The e-media has the unique benefit that the response and reaction rates are so fast. Unlike traditional direct marketing, which relied on the postal delivery, the response on the end of a telephone line, etc. e-media is available every hour of every day, and repeat visits for clarification or for reinforcement, can be undertaken instantly.

9.2 Measurement

In addition to the speed of delivery and reaction, the e-media is highly measurable and trackable. The numbers of visitors, what they look at, where they have come from, where they exit to, etc., are all available to e-marketers, but too great a public use of it may destroy trust as customers feel that they are being watched and that the data is extrapolated in uncontrollable ways.

9.2.1 Online

Online measurements normally revolve around the following metrics:

Page views or 'hits' or 'clicks': this is the traditional measurement, but highly inaccurate. One visitor can view a number of pages in a single session, and may, during the period being examined, view the same page a number of times.

Unique visitors: A more accurate measure, which looks at each computer/user identity and only counts them once in a given period. This can have problems with shared computers, or computers on which certain plug-ins are switched off (such as cookies or JavaScript).

Repeat visits: The best measure of success "repeat visits" rather than clicks? Successful banners that pull in a large number of repeat visitors may appear to burn out. The more successful it is, the fewer eligible clickers remain, because you have already won them[clxvi]. After all, the effectiveness of a website is judged by how your communication with your target audience increases over time. If you want to build a relationship with your visitors because you want them to become a client, a supporter or a partner, they have to visit more than once[clxvii].

There are some tried and tested methods to encourage repeat visits:
- Hold contests or competitions – unfortunately this can attract the disloyal customers
- Use online surveys – listen to what the customers want and then demonstrate that you have heard them (basic trust building)
- Feature customer contributions – people love to be part of a community, and the content will be fresh
- Answer common questions openly – by being open and honest, you will be more likely to build trust and encourage repeat visits
- Offer live online events that will encourage customers back[clxviii]

Most of these activities fall back onto trust building and very visible ethical standpoint, and of course, this will help your offline activities too!

9.2.1.1 Actions

When designing a website, or digital marketing campaign, the interaction must be taken in to consideration, and the methods to bring customers back to relevant information, or to gather information in preparation for another campaign.

9.2.1.2 Click through's

When dealing with affiliate programmes and linking communities, the measurement of click through's (or thru's) is very important as this can form the basis of a remuneration agreement.

Even on ones own site, the click through rate can give an indication of the popularity of a term or image and the referral power that element has. Click through rates can be measured from any interactive electronic media and is akin to the paper coupons of traditional marketing.

9.2.1.3 Open rates

Unlike coupons, and physical letters, e-media can track the 'open' rates – this is the number of people who open the message. This is very important in terms of tracking how attractive the headline or subject line is – how often do you hear that direct mail (on- or offline) heads straight for the bin?

The open rate is only one measure, and there will be a drop off in terms of click through rates as customers discard or file the message. For a well-trusted brand, the open rates should be very high, and if the content has been well targeted, the click through rate should maintain a high level.

9.2.1.4 Tools

There are many tools and tricks to track and measure e-media, but these are technical issues. Some, however, can be seen as trust busting, in that they are seen to spy on the customer. One technique that currently falls between the ethical and unethical practices is the use of a single pixel graphic that sits on a server.

Using html e-mail's, the customer on opening the e-mail will send a request to the server for that image. This provides the open rate statistic, but as with every innovation, there is a counter measure, in this case it is that customers block e-mails from retrieving any external content, rendering some communications completely useless.

9.2.2 Offline

Measurement in an offline world is more difficult as there are more opportunities for mismeasurement. Coupons and vouchers have already been mentioned, and this relies on the customer cutting out and returning or presenting the coupon at the point of purchase.

Another measurement method is in the replies to a campaign, for example the number of telephone calls, or even e-mails following a 'call to action'. Finally, a campaign can generate visits to a shop – of the footfall.

Obviously all of these offline methods can generate or destroy trust through the perceptions of the customer regarding the ethical approach of the company, but it must be recognised that customers have had a longer association with the offline world, its speed and tactics, so trust is probably easier to build and more difficult to destroy in the offline environment.

9.2.2.1 Footfall

Footfall is the physical presence of customers in a shop or at an event. Online, it is possible to identify the unique visitors, whereas a footfall metric is more akin to page impressions on a website and less reliable.

Measuring footfall can be very unobtrusive, with automatic counters at doorways, and customers would happily say that this would not impact their privacy or deem it unethical in anyway. If the shop owner where to mark each customer to determine the uniqueness of the visit, in the way a website can do, that would probably be seen as highly unethical, intrusive and destroy any trust the shoppers would have. Whilst they find cookies and scripted tracking dubious, they accept that more than they would some form of 'branding'.

Another technological method is to monitor customers via close circuit television, possibly automated with facial recognition software. This is another method of unnerving the customer, as this looks like 'Big Brother' watching over the public, as documented by George Orwell in his novel 1984. Again, this would likely be a trustbuster, even if similar methods were acceptable in other walks of life, and especially online.

9.3 Evaluation/ reaction

It is one thing to gather all this information, tracking customers online, offline and as they cross between channels, but the information is only of any use if we can make use of it.

The famous withdrawal of the Safeway ABC loyalty scheme shows that whilst the incentives for building a closer, more understanding relationship with customers is the goal of most marketers, it can only be done if we understand the data we are capturing, why we are capturing it and what we intend to do with it. Indeed the DPA states that we should only collect data if there is a known purpose for it.

Once the data has been captured, the relationship developed, we need to understand the reactions we need to make to build the trust of our customers. It is this that distinguishes whether we understand and relate to the customer, and only then that we can build a rapport that will generate a trusting environment. If, despite the data gathering, we fail to address the issues that our customers tell us matter, and if we fail to relate to them, they will question the need for the data.

9.3.1 Metrics vs. objectives

Obviously all activities need to be planned and developed against objectives to allow their success or failure to be measured and assessed. This should include any ethical brand or trust building.

By setting objectives, any customer feedback can reshape the product, brand or project in a positive way, and new objectives can easily be developed from the new input.

Many projects appear to run without visible objectives, so marketers can then use any feedback as positive, twisting the truth to suit their short term needs. This in turn is likely to reduce trust in the company, as this short-term approach is apparent in the inconsistent approach these companies have to their dealings with their customers, be that on- or offline or a mixture of the two.

10. Evaluation

10.1 Results

If a company is investing in new technology, or in a new approach to a marketplace, such as trying to be ethical in a new sector, or to build trust, the results of this must be evaluated to establish whether it has been successful.

For the measurement of ethics and trust, it is difficult to have an empirical formula to provide the answers of whether the campaign or action has succeeded. But this can also be seen as a positive thing, in that in setting up the campaign, we can define how we will be measured against our objectives.

In most cases the measures of ethics and trust manifest themselves in increased loyalty (which is measurable), in a reduction in legal action (measurable, but undesirable) and the recovery of customer 'faith' after a problem (not easily measured and equally undesirable).

As has been reinforced a number of times in this book, the results can only be compared against the original objectives of the campaign, and these should always include an element of trust building and an ethics check.

10.2 Return On Investment (ROI)

In modern business, everything seems to be converted into financial benefits, and as such most market campaigns must have a return on investment (ROI) target. Whilst this is not disputed – in terms of trust building or ethical branding, this is a longer-term proposition and as such, returns will be longer in coming.

If a company were to undertake a trust building activity, for example, it would be unwise to stop any product or service marketing through online or traditional channels, which does dilute the measurable returns of the campaign. This is one reason that it is better to incorporate an element of ethics and trust building into the mainstream campaigns being carried out, and using the uplift in ROI over a benchmark as the ROI in terms of the objectives of trust and ethics.

10.3 Measurement

Other measurement, as has been identified, could be the customer loyalty, although this differs widely between industry sectors. Again, by setting the objectives and getting the buy in for them in advance will help track the success of the action.

Of course, it would be far easier to measure the reverse – a brand busting campaign, as the effects of this would be almost immediate, and therefore the returns (or lack of them) quite severe.

11.   Future

11.1 Futurologists

Most of the major technology companies employ 'futurologists' who's job it is to predict future technology, socio-demographic and fashion trends. It sounds like something out of a Science Fiction series, and you would expect these people to be the boring, scientific types. Indeed, some maybe so, but they are generally very ordinary, albeit highly creative and imaginative people.

Predicting the future is difficult enough when just looking at the technology. Moore's Law which is widely associated with the claim that computing power at fixed cost is doubling every 18 months, and demonstrates the dynamic nature of that market.

> The observation made in 1965 by Gordon Moore, co-founder of Intel, that the number of transistors per square inch on integrated circuits had doubled every year since the integrated circuit was invented. Moore predicted that this trend would continue for the foreseeable future. In subsequent years, the pace slowed down a bit, but data density has doubled approximately every 18 months, and this is the current definition of Moore's Law, which Moore himself has blessed. Most experts, including Moore himself, expect Moore's Law to hold for at least another two decades[clxix].

Fashion and trends in general are obviously more difficult to predict, making the whole subject imprecise. Timelines are distorted and seemingly ever decreasing, and the take up by the public is a factor that is the most difficult to determine.

11.2 Markets

At the beginning of the Eighties, who would have thought that the East bloc regimes would crumble, and that in the early twenty-first century the EU would expand into some of those countries?

Call centres moving to India, production to China, etc., are all indications that we live in a global economy, made increasingly smaller thanks to technology. This also means that our home markets are changing, for example the shift to service industries in the UK, coupled with nearly full employment in 2004, resulting in a buoyant economy, and happier citizens. As the production costs for some goods reduce, partly because of using cheaper labour, so these products become more widely accessible, driving demand.

So far so good. But as we expand into other markets, we are also exposed to different ethical views and restrictions. We can no longer impose our own ethics on the indigenous populations of the world, as the Empire builders of the Nineteenth century did. With e-media, we will be exposed to such markets, whether we planned to target them or not. The future of ethical marketing is in a homogenised standard ethic that may push boundaries in some countries, and may be seen a prudish in others, but will cause least offence.

External factors may also play a part, with world trade negotiations trying to open up the world, protectionism hindering this, and increasingly, environmental and social factors playing an increasing role. This is most evident following the campaign that surrounded Naomi Klein's book 'No Logo' in which she highlighted the socially abhorrent practices of many Western clothing manufacturers in the Far East, singling Nike out and causing a massive backlash.

11.3 Ethics

It is conceivable that our ethical perceptions will alter over the next fifty to hundred years, thus some of the possible infringements we identify today will become acceptable in the future. Not even the professional futurologists can predict these changes, so we must base our actions on today's benchmarks.

With the increasing pace of life, and the demand for more of our customer's time and money, information will become a valuable resource that companies (and hopefully individuals) will fight hard to keep confidential. Customers, with less free time to acknowledge advertisements, will relish properly targeted and relevant messages. This is bound to shape future ethics.

11.3.1 Political correctness

Over the last twenty years we have seen an increase in politically correct (PC) behaviour by governments and companies, leading to an almost laughable situation where age-old terms are now no longer acceptable.

Whilst we do not want to return to the bigoted ways of the past, ready adoption of a 'totally PC' culture, whilst ethically sound, could lead to the market no longer taking the company or brand seriously. We now see a number of advertisements making fun of non-PC attitudes, or conversely of overly PC attitudes, both now deemed laughable.

11.3.2 Rise in fundamentalism

Even if you manage to define a workable, acceptable medium between the ethical views of all your various customers, considering political correctness, you may still have a problem.

Fundamentalism is on the increase around the world. It used to be the domain of religious cults and Islamic hardliners, but has now spread to other religions and pseudo-terrorist organisations, such as animal rights protesters. Again, using the example of Nike with there product 'design' on the back of a pair of training shoes that was deemed to look like the Arabic word for 'Allah', offending Muslims and creating yet another Nike backlash.

In the UK, the musical 'Jerry Springer' has been boycotted by Christian groups because of its anti-Christian message, and the BBC vilified for screening the musical on TV. And in Birmingham, a play about Sikhs was forced to close thanks to an angry mob threatening organisers and playgoers in 2004.

All these factors mean that your ethical stance is increasingly becoming a major issue in the way you conduct your business, and the way that you interact with your public, around the globe.

11.4 Media

The media landscape has changed remarkably over the last twenty years, with an increase in the number of channels to customers, and the number of options within those channels. When I first saw the Internet in 1992, my view was that this was a great medium for information, but that I failed to see how anyone could make any money from it. Happily I was wrong about that prediction, I hope that admission does not negate what is written in this chapter.

The media, especially e-media will play an increasingly important role over the next ten or twenty years, as the access to information, and therefore to retail opportunities increase. We are likely to reach saturation point very soon, but it is also likely that as we reach it, a new technology or process will sort things out so that our brains can catch up.

Indices

Table of Tables

Table of Figures

Subject Index

References

Chapter 1

[i] Source: http://www.corporate-citizenship.co.uk

[ii] Definition from the National Art Education Association Conference – 1996

[iii] Kerin, R.A., Varadarajan, P.R., and Peterson, R.A. - "First-Mover Advantage: A Synthesis, Conceptual Framework, and Research Propositions" Journal of Marketing, 56 (October 1992), 33-52.

[iv] Entine, J. - Taboo: Why Black Athletes Dominate Sport and Why Were Afraid to Talk About It, 1996

[v] McClenahen, J.S. and Jusko, J. - "Doing IT E-Right." Industry Week 249.13 (2000): 13-15

[vi] Klein, N. - No Logo (2000). Flamingo Publishers, London

[vii] Source: http://www.ibilbilo.org

[viii] Brand, S. - *The Media Lab: Inventing the Future at MIT.* Penguin (1988).

[ix] Brand, S. - *The Media Lab: Inventing the Future at MIT.* Penguin (1988).

[x] Godin, S. - Permission Marketing – Turning strangers into friends, and friends into customers (1999 – Simon & Schuster)

[xi] Kavali, S G., Tzokas, N.X., Saren, M.J. - Relationship marketing as an ethical approach: philosophical & managerial considerations – Management Decision 37/7 1999 Page 575

Chapter 2

[xii] From http://chiron.valdosta.edu/whuitt/col/cogsys/piaget.html

[xiii] Rotter, J. from http://www.dushkin.com/connectext/psy/ch11/survey11.mhtml (1966)

[xiv] Heinze, Dr. P. - Psychopathy, Machiavellianism and Ethics: A View of Business Ethics from a Clinical Psychology Perspective from http://m05.cgpublisher.com/proposals/191/index_html (2005)

[xv] European Association of Communications Agencies Code of Ethics - 2005

[xvi] Sindell, K. - Loyalty Marketing for the Internet Age (2000)

[xvii] Sindell, K. - Loyalty Marketing for the Internet Age (2000)

[xviii] CACI information services 2004 (from the Marketing Pocket Book 2005 – WARC) Page 20-21

[xix] Sindell, K. - Loyalty Marketing for the Internet Age (2000)

[xx] Armstrong, R.W., Stening, B.W., Ryans, J.K., Marks, L., and Mayo, M. – International Marketing Ethics: Problems Encountered by Australian Firms. International Marketing Ethics (1999) Page 5

[xxi] A study conducted by Arthur Andersen in 2001

[xxii] A Harris study in 2003 source .Net magazine

[xxiii] BBC News, November 2004

[xxiv] From Business Life Magazine (Oct 1996)

[xxv] From a presentation to the IABC by Nick Winkfield, May 2005

[xxvi] From http://www.iep.utm.edu/e/ethics.htm

[xxvii] Baker, J. - Marketing Ethics (2001) Page 126

[xxviii] Laczniak, G.R. & Murphy, P.E. - Ethical Marketing Decisions: The Higher Road. 1993 Page 49-51

Chapter 3

[xxix] From http://www.rdtrustedbrands.com 2005

[xxx] Senia, A. - Gain Customers' Trust and Increase Online Sales. From the June 23, 2000 issue of VARBusiness

[xxxi] Urban, G.L., Sultan, F., Qualls, W.J. – Placing Trust at the Center of Your Internet Strategy. Sloan Management Review. Fall 2000 Page 40

[xxxii] Blau, P. (1964). Exchange and power in social life. New York: Wiley; Rotter, J. B. (1967) 'A new scale for the measurement of interpersonal trust', Journal of Personality, Vol. 35, No. 4, pp. 651–665. 40. - Building Trust To Develop Competitive Advantage In E-business Relationships. By: Warrington, T.B.; Abgrab, N. J.; Caldwell, H.M. - Competitiveness Review, 2000, Vol. 10 Issue 2, p160, 9p;

[xxxiii] Chen and Yeager, 2002 – Source: Ignatiadis, I., Svirskas, A., Roberts, R., Tarabanis, K.. International Journal of Networking & Virtual Organisations; 2006, Vol. 3 Issue 4, p395-411, 17p

[xxxiv] Abdul-Rahman, A. & Hailes, S. - A Distributed Trust Model. Dissertation for Department of Computer Science, University College London, 1997

[xxxv] Blois, K.J. - Trust in Business to Business Relationships: An Evaluation of its Status – Journal of Management Studies 36:2 March 1999 Page 205

[xxxvi] Corby, M.J. - The Case for Privacy. Information Systems Security May/June 2002 Page 9

[xxxvii] Mand, 1998; Guly, 1998; from Prabhaker, P.R. – Who owns the online consumer? Journal of Consumer Marketing Vol.17 No.2 2000

[xxxviii] Barber, B. - The logic and limits of trust. New Brunswick, NJ: Rutgers University Press. 1983.

[xxxix] Abdul-Rahman, A. & Hailes, S. - A Distributed Trust Model. Dissertation for Department of Computer Science, University College London, 1997

[xl] McKean, J. - Customer Are People 2002 Page. 2

[xli] McKean, J. - Customer Are People 2002 Page. 10

[xlii] Urban, G.L., Sultan, F., Qualls, W.J. – Placing Trust at the Center of Your Internet Strategy. Sloan Management Review. Fall 2000 Page 40

[xliii] Birkhofer, B., Schoegel, M., Tomczak, T. – Transaction- and Trust-Based Strategies in E-commerce – a Conceptual Approach. Electronic Commerce & Marketing Vol. 10 No. 3 2000 Page 173

[xliv] Warrington, T.B., Abgrab, N.J., Caldwell, H.M. – Building Trust to Develop Competitive Advantage in E-Business Relationships. CR Vol.10(2), 2000 Page 160
[xlv] Goldstein, D. - Establishing e-trust. The Magazine for Magazine Management. Vol.30, Issue 1 2001 Page 178
[xlvi] Carrigan, M. - "Is there such a thing as an ethical consumer?" Journal: Strategic Direction. Year: 2003 Volume: 19 Issue: 6 Page: 28 - 30
[xlvii] Folkes, V.S. & Kamins M.A. - Effects of Information about Firms' Ethical and Unethical Actions on Consumers' Attitudes. Journal of Consumer Psychology, Vol. 8, No. 3, Ethical Trade-Offs in Consumer Decision Making (1999), pp. 243-259
[xlviii] McKean, J. - Customer Are People 2002 Page. 127
[xlix] Ali, H. and Birley, S. - The Role of Trust in the Marketing Activities of Entrepreneurs Establishing New Ventures. Journal of Marketing Management. 1998, 14, Page 752
[l] Ali, H. and Birley, S. - The Role of Trust in the Marketing Activities of Entrepreneurs Establishing New Ventures. Journal of Marketing Management. 1998
[li] Urban, G.L., Sultan, F., Qualls, W.J. – Placing Trust at the Center of Your Internet Strategy. Sloan Management Review. Fall 2000 Page 48
[lii] Weber, L.R. & Carter, A.I. - The Social Construction of Trust. Springer Science+Business Media 2002
[liii] Moran, M. - Brand and Trust on the Internet. Chemical Week. 1999 Page 14
[liv] Ali, H. and Birley, S. - The Role of Trust in the Marketing Activities of Entrepreneurs Establishing New Ventures. Journal of Marketing Management. 1998, 14, Page 750
[lv] Ali, H. and Birley, S. - The Role of Trust in the Marketing Activities of Entrepreneurs Establishing New Ventures. Journal of Marketing Management. 1998, 14, Page 7512
[lvi] Abdul-Rahman, A. & Hailes, S. - A Distributed Trust Model. Dissertation for Department of Computer Science, University College London, 1997
[lvii] Luhmann, N. - Trust and Power. John Wiley & Sons Inc (May 1982)
[lviii] Adaptation of the model to understand e-Commerce trust by Jonathan Reynolds – e-Commerce a critical review in the International Journal of Retail & Distribution Management Vol 28 No. 10 2000 Page 426 (Poole, T. 2005) - original 1999 Studio Archetype & Cheskin Research
[lix] Abdul-Rahman, A. & Hailes, S. - A Distributed Trust Model. Dissertation for Department of Computer Science, University College London, 1997
[lx] Misztal, B.A. - Trust in Modern Societies: The Search for the Bases of Social Order. Polity Press (December 1995)
[lxi] Abdul-Rahman, A. & Hailes, S. - A Distributed Trust Model. Dissertation for Department of Computer Science, University College London, 1997
[lxii] Spremann, K. (2000): Portfoliomanagement, Munich, from Liechtensteiner Vaterland article - 22 October 2005
[lxiii] Nycum, T.M. - 2000, Source: Nakra, P. Consumer privacy rights: CPR and the age of the Internet. Management Decision 39/4 2001
[lxiv] Nakra, P. - Consumer privacy rights: CPR and the age of the Internet. Management Decision 39/4 2001 Page 276
[lxv] Urban, G.L., Sultan, F., Qualls, W.J. – Placing Trust at the Center of Your Internet Strategy. Sloan Management Review. Fall 2000 Page 46
[lxvi] Urban, G.L., Sultan, F., Qualls, W.J. – Placing Trust at the Center of Your Internet Strategy. Sloan Management Review. Fall 2000 Page 46
[lxvii] Cuthbertson, R. – Loyalty Marketing Online: Can platonic relationship work? From http://www.loyalty4profit.com 2000 Page 1
[lxviii] Prabhaker, P.R. – Who owns the online consumer? Journal of Consumer Marketing Vol.17 No.2 2000. Page 160
[lxix] World Economic Forum, January 2003 Part 1. From http://www.weforum.org/site/hompublic.hsf/Content
[lxx] Jevons, C. and Gabbott, M – Trust, Brand Equity and Brand Reality in Internet Business Relationships: An Interdisciplinary Approach. Journal of Marketing Management. 16. 2000 Page 625
[lxxi] Nakra, P. - Consumer privacy rights: CPR and the age of the Internet. Management Decision 39/4 2001 Page 277
[lxxii] McKnight & Chervany, from Abdul-Rahman, A. & Hailes, S. - A Distributed Trust Model. Dissertation for Department of Computer Science, University College London, 1997
[lxxiii] Abdul-Rahman, A. & Hailes, S. - A Distributed Trust Model. Dissertation for Department of Computer Science, University College London, 1997
[lxxiv] Randall, V. - Dysfunctional marketing fails – Communication World, Vol.17 No.1 1999 Page 5, from Rich, M.K., Are we losing trust through technology? Journal of Business & Industrial Marketing. Vol.17 No.2/3 2002 Page 216
[lxxv] Rich, M.K. - Are we losing trust through technology? Journal of Business & Industrial Marketing. Vol.17 No.2/3 2002 Page 216
[lxxvi] Hunt, S., Wood, V. & Chonko, L. – Corporate ethical values and organizational commitment in marketing. Journal of Marketing, Vol.53, No.3 1989 pp79-91 – from Rich, M.K., Are we losing trust through technology? Journal of Business & Industrial Marketing. Vol.17 No.2/3 2002 Page 220

[lxxvii] Rich, M.K. - Are we losing trust through technology? Journal of Business & Industrial Marketing. Vol.17 No.2/3 2002 Page 220

[lxxviii] Cannon, D.A. - The Ethics of Database Marketing – The Information Management Journal. May/June 2002. Page 42

[lxxix] Corby, M.J. - The Case for Privacy. Information Systems Security May/June 2002 Page 12

[lxxx] Kappelman, L.A. - Working In The Global Village. InformationWeek March 20, 2000. Page 150

[lxxxi] Cannon, D.A. - The Ethics of Database Marketing – The Information Management Journal. May/June 2002. Page 43

[lxxxii] Urban, G.L., Sultan, F., Qualls, W.J. – Placing Trust at the Center of Your Internet Strategy. Sloan Management Review. Fall 2000 Page 47

[lxxxiii] Barber (1983) from Abdul-Rahman. A. & Hailes, S. - A Distributed Trust Model. Dissertation for Department of Computer Science, University College London, 1997)

[lxxxiv] From http://www.rdtrustedbrands.com 2005

[lxxxv] A classification matrix of trust research in relationships between individuals and/or organisations. Svensson, G. - Management Decision 39/6 (2001) Page 432

[lxxxvi] English, P. – http://www.paulenglish.com, 2004

[lxxxvii] Kotler, P. - Marketing Management 11th Edition, Prentice Hall 2003.

[lxxxviii] Kerin, R A., P. R Varadarajan, and R A. Peterson - "First-Mover Advantage: A Synthesis, Conceptual Framework, and Research Propositions," Journal of Marketing, 56 (October 1992), 33-52.

[lxxxix] Klein, N. - No Logo– Flamingo – HarperCollins Publishers 2001

[xc] Brennan, M. - Is there more to ethical marketing than marketing ethics? Marketing Bulletin, (1991), 2, 8-17

[xci] Peters, T.J. & Waterman, R.H. - In Search of Excellence – Lessons from America's Best-run Companies. 1993 – HarperCollins Publishers

[xcii] Smith, P.R. - Marketing Communications – an integrated approach 2nd Edition. 1993

[xciii] Smith, P.R. - Marketing Communications – an integrated approach 2nd Edition. 1993

[xciv] Business Impact Review Group comprises: BAA, BUPA, Cap Gemini Ernst & Young, Carillion, Coca-Cola GB, CIS, Flag, GUS, HBOS, Jaguar, EDF Energy (formerly London Electricity Group), Marks & Spencer, Nestle, Orange, Powergen, Sainsbury's Supermarkets Ltd., Severn Trent, Thames Water, United Utilities, Zurich UK. Details on http://www.bitc.org.uk

[xcv] Peter and Olson 1987 – from Brennan, M. - Is there more to ethical marketing than marketing ethics? Marketing Bulletin, (1991)

[xcvi] Baker, M.J. Editor - The Marketing Book 1998

[xcvii] Baker, M.J. Editor - The Marketing Book 1998

[xcviii] Smith, P.R. - Marketing Communications – an integrated approach 2nd Edition. 1993

[xcix] McClenahen, J.S. and Jusko, J. - "Doing IT E-Right." Industry Week 249.13 (2000): 13-15

[c] Bibb, S. & Kourdi, J. - Trust Matters. 2004. Page 7

[ci] Kettle, M. - We can't just blame our lack of trust on Tony Blair's 'lies' – Guardian Newspaper Saturday December 30, 2006

[cii] Plato - Translated by Lee, D. The Republic. 1974

[ciii] Adapted from Porter, M. by Poole, T. - Data Privacy & The Marketing Art Of The Opt-In, 2003

[civ] From Maslow, A. - adapted Poole, 2004

[cv] Anon

[cvi] Salkever, A. - Strategies for Winning the War on Spam. BusinessWeek AUGUST 20, 2002

[cvii] From http://www.silicon.com, 2002

[cviii] From mailmsg.com

[cix] Salkever, A. - Strategies for Winning the War on Spam. BusinessWeek AUGUST 20, 2002

[cx] BBC News report Jul 2004

[cxi] Fox, S. - Plugged In: Devious Variations on an Old E-Mail Scam - PCWorld magazine June 26, 2003

[cxii] BBC News, 18/11/04

[cxiii] Maurer, S.D. & Zugelder, M.T. - Journal of High Technology Management Research; Autumn 2000, Vol. 11 Issue 2, p155, 20p

[cxiv] Goff, L. - Computerworld 1998

[cxv] From Evershed e80 newsletter – 10/03/04 (http://www.evershed.com)

[cxvi] From http://www.fool.co.uk

[cxvii] Smith, P.R. - Marketing Communications – an integrated approach 2nd Ed. 1998. Page 7

Chapter 4

[cxviii] Fill, C. - Marketing Communications – contexts, contents and strategies. 2d Ed. 1999. Page 3

[cxix] Based on Schramm, W. (1995) and Shannon & Weaver (1962) – from Fill, C. - Marketing Communications – contexts, contents and strategies, 2nd Ed. 1999 Page 24

[cxx] Brower, M., and Leon, W. – "Practical Advice from the Union of Concerned Scientists" http://www.ucsusa.org/publications/guide.ch1.html

[cxxi] Poole, T.F. 2005 - based on a concept by Godin, S.
[cxxii] Godin, S. - Permission Marketing – Turning strangers into friends, and friends into customers (1999 – Simon & Schuster)
[cxxiii] Stone 1925 – from Fill, C. - Marketing Communications – context, contents and strategies. 2nd Ed. 1999 Page 266
[cxxiv] From Smith, P.R. - Marketing Communications – an integrated approach. 2nd Ed. 1998. Page 94. Models – AIDA (Strong, E.K. 1925); Lavidge & Steiner 1961; Adoption (Rogers, E.M. 1961); DAGMAR (Colley, R.H. 1961); Howard & Sheth (1969, excerpt)
[cxxv] Rosen, R.G. - Innovation Best Practices in the USA presentation – IDM 2005
[cxxvi] Poole, T.F. 2005
[cxxvii] Rake, M. - Corporate ethics travel well. Companies That Count 2005. April 3rd 2005
[cxxviii] From http://www.ftse.com/ftse4good/
[cxxix] From Fill, C. - Marketing Communications – context, contents and strategies. 2nd Ed. 1999 Page 53
[cxxx] MacDonald, M. - Marketing Plans – How to prepare the, how to use them. 4th Ed. 1999. Page 302
[cxxxi] Bell, A. - Ten Steps to SMART objectives. 2003
[cxxxii] Man in the chair advert - McGraw-Hill
[cxxxiii] Stefansson, V. - "Discovery", 1964
[cxxxiv] Cosby, W.
[cxxxv] Nielsen, J. – http://www.useit.com
[cxxxvi] Nielsen, J. – http://www.useit.com

Chapter 5
[cxxxvii] From the Plain English Campaign newsletter 8/4/04
[cxxxviii] From The Times, Thursday 15th November 1990. Page 14/15

Chapter 6
[cxxxix] From Sun Tzu – Strategies for Marketing by Michaelson & Michaelson, 2004 Page 180
[cxl] Godin, S. - Permission Marketing – Turning strangers into friends, and friends into customers (1999 – Simon & Schuster)
[cxli] Goldstein, D. - Establishing e-trust. The Magazine for Magazine Management. Vol.30, Issue 1 2001
[cxlii] Kolko, J. & Strohm, C.Q. - Who Has Given Up The Internet? January 14, 2004
[cxliii] Urban, G.L., Sultan, F., Qualls, W.J. – Placing Trust at the Center of Your Internet Strategy. Sloan Management Review. Fall 2000 Page 40
[cxliv] Urban, G.L., Sultan, F., Qualls, W.J. – Placing Trust at the Center of Your Internet Strategy. Sloan Management Review. Fall 2000 Page 40
[cxlv] Urban, G.L., Sultan, F., Qualls, W.J. – Placing Trust at the Center of Your Internet Strategy. Sloan Management Review. Fall 2000 Page 40
[cxlvi] Urban, G.L., Sultan, F., Qualls, W.J. – Placing Trust at the Center of Your Internet Strategy. Sloan Management Review. Fall 2000 Page 40
[cxlvii] From http://www.cellular .co.za/news/news_2004/may/0500404-uk_sms_traffic_continues_to_rise.htm

Chapter 8
[cxlviii] Story from BBC NEWS: http://news.bbc.co.uk/go/pr/fr/-/1/hi/technology/4400335.stm Published: 2005/04/01
[cxlix] From The Spamhouse Project (spamhouse.org) correct as at 23 April 2005
[cl] from the office of the Data Registrar - http://www.ico.gov.uk/
[cli] CAN-SPAM Act of 2003 (Pub. L. 108-187, S. 877) from http://www.spamlaws.com/federal/summ108.shtml
[clii] From http://www.whitehouse.gov/news/releases/2003/12/20031216-4.html
[cliii] From http://www.newstarget.com/001412.html CAN-SPAM legislation proving useless against spam 24/04/2005
[cliv] From http://www.newstarget.com/001122.html Compliance with CAN-SPAM fast approaches zero; only a technical solution can halt spam 24/04/2005
[clv] From http://www.arialsoftware.com/whitepapers/CANSPAMComplianceAudit2004.pdf
[clvi] From http://www.can-spamcompliance.com/canspam.html
[clvii] Source: U.S. Census Bureau 2001
[clviii] Source: Office of National Statistics 2004
[clix] Source: Office of National Statistics 2004
[clx] Source: Royal National Institute for the Blind 2004
[clxi] Source: Employers Forum on Disability
[clxii] Definition from http://www.section508.gov

Chapter 9
[clxiii] From http://www.kuleuven.ac.be/facdep/social/com/english/projects/elokaleoverheid.htm
[clxiv] Hayward, W.G. & Tong, K.K. - Effects of language on website usage with bilingual users - Proceedings of the 9th Annual Conference on Human-Computer Interaction – Blackwell Publishers (2001)

[clxv] Gillham, R. & Maroto, J. - Cross cultural interactive marketing: the implications of culture in Website usability'. (November 2003) New Media Knowledge. Online at: http://www.nmk.co.uk/article/2003/09/01/localisation
[clxvi] BabyGear.com's Preston Bealle on Targeted Media Buying and Why Branding is an "Evil" Word – Marketing Sherpa. Jun 09, 2000
[clxvii] Steve Hall – http://www.o-a.com/archive/1997/August/0121.html
[clxviii] From http://www.bcentral.co.uk/marketing/onlinemarketing/building-a-sticky-website.mspx

Chapter 11
[clxix] From Webopedia.com